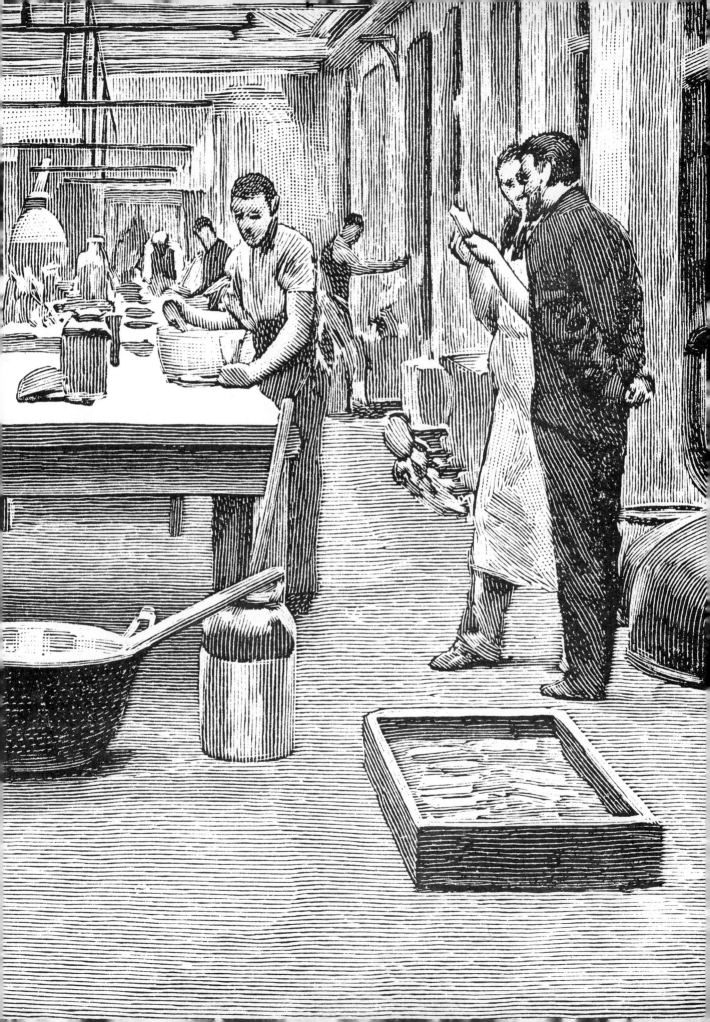

History Eye-witness

Inventors

Norman Wymer

Silver Burdett Company

Acknowledgements

The items illustrated on the following pages are reproduced by kind permission of the President and Council of The Royal College of Surgeons of England 31, 32, 33 top, 33 bottom.

Photographs

City of Aberdeen County Library 30–31; BBC, London 22; BBC Hulton Picture Library, London 46, 47 top, 48 top, 48 bottom, 52, 61 top right, 64, 66, 67 top right, 70 left, 85; British Airways, London 60–61, 90; British Museum, London 11 top, 55 left; British Rail, London 17; Capital Radio, London 47 bottom; Crown Copyright, Science Museum, London 14 bottom, 63; E.M.I. Electronics, London 67 top left; Glaxo Operations U.K., Greenford 71; Hamlyn Group Picture Library 41 top right; Hamlyn Group Picture Library – Charles Pocklington 21; Imperial War Museum, London 72, 74, 76 top, 76 bottom left, 76 bottom right, 86 top, 86 bottom; Dr W. Kolff 79, 80, 82 top, 82 bottom, 83 top; Linotype-Paul, London 11 bottom right; London Weekend Television 67 bottom; Manpower Services Commission, London 23; Mansell Collection, London front and back endpapers, 8, 11 bottom left, 61 top left; Marconi Electronics, Chelmsford 45; Marconi Radar Systems, Chelmsford 77 top left, 77 top right, 77 bottom; St. Mary's Hospital Medical School, London 34, 35, 53, 69, 70 right; N.A.S.A., Washington, D.C. 88, 89; Popperfoto, London 29; The Post Office, London 41 top left, 41 upper centre left, 41 upper centre right, 41 lower centre, 41 bottom left, 41 bottom right; Royal College of Surgeons, London 31, 32, 33 top, 33 bottom; Science Museum, London 13 left, 13 right, 14 top, 15, 24 left, 24 right, 27; Syndication International, London 91; U.S. Department of the Interior, National Park Service, Edison National Park Service, Edison National Historic Site, West Orange, New Jersey 25; Wright State University, Dayton, Ohio 55 right; Norman Wymer 39, 40, 83 bottom.

Published 1981 by
The Hamlyn Publishing Group Limited
London · New York · Sydney · Toronto
Astronaut House, Feltham, Middlesex, England

Published in the United States by
Silver Burdett Company, Morristown, N.J.
1982 Printing

ISBN 0-382-06666-9

Library of Congress
Catalog Card No. 82-50398

Illustrations by Jeff Burns, Mike Codd, Peter Dennis and Roger Full Industrial Arts Studio.

Contents

Johannes Gutenberg

The art of printing 1455

One of the most important inventions of any age was the invention of printing, in the fifteenth century. Before that time all books were written by hand with quill pens, made from the stems of birds' feathers. They were generally written by monks, and sometimes 'scribes' were employed to copy a manuscript. It might take months or years to make a single copy. The work was so slow and laborious that very few copies of any book were produced, and they were mainly for priests or scholars.

Ordinary people seldom had a chance to read a book before the days of printing.

In very early times the Chinese, Romans and others had found ways of stamping words using wood or clay blocks, but this elementary method of printing could be used only for short inscriptions or for such purposes as stamping titles on the leather bindings of books. The Chinese also invented a method of printing with movable type, but it was impractical for the Chinese language which has thousands of characters.

The man who first invented a practical method of printing was a German named Johannes Gutenberg, who was born in Mainz in about 1397. His father, an aristocrat, was one of the city's leading officials and Master of the Mint.

Gutenberg, as a boy, often went to the Mint and watched the goldsmiths stamp the letters and figures on the coins with metal punches – and their work intrigued him.

He also spent much time in the monasteries of Mainz, where he watched the monks writing the Bible – a work that took many years to complete. Gutenberg studied the precious handwritten books in the monastery libraries and felt that there must be a way to ease the work of the scribes. He thought of the coin-makers' stamps, and a germ of an idea came to his mind. He wondered if it might be possible to copy the script of the monks by some form of 'artificial writing'.

The first experiments

Inspired by the craftsmen at the Mint, Gutenberg was apprenticed to a goldsmith and became a skilful metal-worker.

In 1428 an uprising of workers against aristocratic families forced him to leave Mainz. Gutenberg, who was now about 31, moved to Strasbourg, and there he began to experiment with new technical processes for making various articles in metal.

Through these experiments, he conceived the

Below: A library of chained books. When manuscripts were written by hand, and in the early days of printing, books were so rare that they were very precious, and so they were often chained to the shelves to prevent people stealing them. The chained library in Hereford Cathedral dates back to the Middle Ages.

idea of printing by means of movable metal type – a process whereby the letters of the alphabet are cast individually and then assembled to frame words.

Gutenberg aimed to imitate the style of writing used by the monks so that the printed text would look exactly like the original hand-written script.

As Gutenberg had no money to develop his invention, he formed a partnership with a German named Andreas Dritzehen and two other men. They gave Gutenberg 500 guilders and, in return, he agreed to teach them his 'secret art'.

Gutenberg bought lead for the type and started to construct some kind of printing apparatus. He was making good progress.

Then suddenly Andreas Dritzehen died. His two brothers – worthless men – demanded to be taken into partnership in the place of Andreas. Gutenberg refused. Fearing that the brothers might learn his secret and steal his invention, he dismantled his equipment and his work came to a temporary halt.

For ten years Gutenberg tried in vain to borrow money to start afresh. In desperation, he left Strasbourg and returned to Mainz to try his luck there. In Mainz he confided his secret to a lawyer named Fust and persuaded him to provide the money. Fust lent Gutenberg 800 guilders, charging him interest at six per cent.

Before printing came to Europe, in the late 1300s, books were laboriously hand-written. Printing originated in China; the earliest surviving printed book dates from 868 A.D. The Chinese first began to use movable type between 1040 and 1050 A.D.

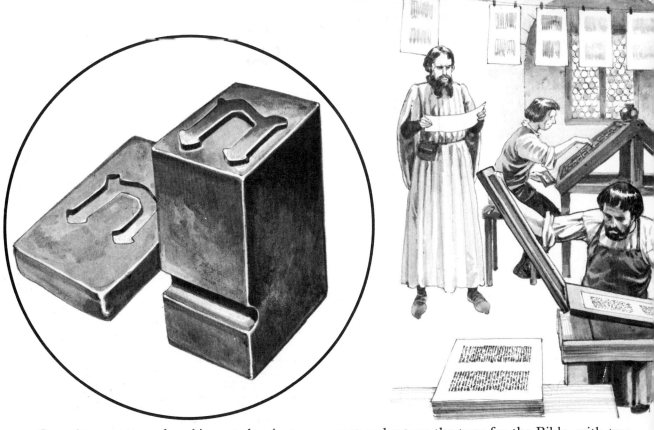

Gutenberg set to work and invented an instrument for casting the letters. For each letter, he made a steel punch and then stamped it into a block of copper to form a die. This die was placed in the casting instrument, and molten metal was poured in. When the metal set, sticks formed and each stick bore a letter at the end in relief – like the letters on a typewriter. Gutenberg also designed a printing press.

Gutenberg wanted to print the Bible in Latin, but he had now spent Fust's loan and he had no money to buy the expensive printing materials. Besides the lead for the type, he needed special ink; hand-made paper, manufactured from rags; and costly vellum, for which the hides of 10,000 calves would be required. On top of these heavy expenses, Gutenberg also had to pay for the manufacture of his printing press.

Gutenberg's Bible

Gutenberg asked Fust for a further loan. Fust refused. He had a better idea – one of advantage to himself. The cunning lawyer, seeing a chance to make a fortune, proposed that he and Gutenberg form a business partnership 'for printing books' and share the profits. Fust offered to invest 800 guilders in the business and to pay the printing costs. Gutenberg accepted his terms gladly.

When the printing press had been made and the materials obtained, Gutenberg proceeded to cast and set up the type for the Bible, with two columns to a page and 42 lines to a column. The work took three years. At last, the book was ready for printing.

Fust now determined to destroy Gutenberg. He demanded the immediate repayment of his original loan of 800 guilders, together with the accumulated interest, which amounted to more than 2,000 guilders. As Gutenberg was unable to repay the money, Fust seized his printing apparatus and took over the business.

In 1455 two hundred copies of the famous 'Gutenberg Bible' were printed – and Fust took all the money from the sales. Gutenberg gained nothing from his valuable invention and was financially ruined. He died, destitute and forgotten, in 1468.

But the world benefited. A printer could print in one day more reading matter than a scribe could write in a year – and he could print any number of copies. As a result, the publishing of books for the public began – and a great new field for learning was opened up.

Books were printed by Gutenberg's process for nearly 500 years – until mechanical methods were introduced in the present century.

In Mainz, there is a Gutenberg Museum which houses a copy of his Bible, a model of his workshop and his printing apparatus, and many other treasures, and opposite the museum is a statue of the great inventor.

Top left: Dies used for individual letters.

Above: The printing press in use in Gutenberg's workshop.

Below: Illustration from a manuscript of 1324, printed from wood and metallic blocks which appeared in one of the first printed books in Europe, in 1430.

Top right: A page from the Gutenberg Bible.

Right: A Linotype 794 Linecaster. The Linotype was invented by Ottmar Mergenthaler, and first used by the *New York Tribune*.

George Stephenson

The first railways 1825

Before the days of railways, coaches drawn by horses were the main form of public transport. The coaches were very uncomfortable and over-crowded with passengers. Some passengers were packed inside like sardines in a tin; others sat outside in the wind, rain and cold of winter.

There were no tarmac roads. The coaches bumped along tracks riddled with ruts and pot-holes. Travelling was very hazardous. A wheel might catch in a rut and turn a coach over – or highwaymen might hold up a coach with pistols and rob the passengers.

People never travelled long distances unless their journey was essential. It could take days to travel between towns far apart. A long-distance journey was made in 'stages', and travellers spent the night at inns at the stopping places.

George Stephenson, son of a coal miner, built the first railways. He was born in 1781 in a mining village near Newcastle. His parents were too poor to send him to school and, as a boy, George worked in a mine, picking stones out of coal, for a wage of sixpence a day.

At the colliery his father tended an old steam engine used for pumping water out of the mine. This was the kind of job George wanted. He went to another colliery and worked as a mech-anic. Gradually he climbed the ladder to better jobs until, at the age of 17, he was given charge of an engine.

Stephenson took a great pride in his engine; he dismantled it and studied its workings. He was fired with an ambition to become an engineer like James Watt, the inventor of the steam engine.

Highwaymen were a common threat to coach travellers. One of the most notorious characters was Dick Turpin, who terrorized the London to York route and was hanged at York in 1739.

His lack of education was a handicap. He would need to study the theoretical side of engineering, but he could neither read nor write. Stephenson overcame this obstacle. In the evenings after work, a young schoolmaster taught him reading, writing and arithmetic for a penny a lesson.

The moving engine

Though he received no practical training, Stephenson became a skilful engineer. His great opportunity came at 33, by then married with a son named Robert. Stephenson was in charge of the colliery's stationary engines, used for drawing up coal from the deep pits. He also supervised the transport of the coal from the colliery to the port for shipment to the customers.

Machinery was then beginning to take the place of manual labour, and factories were being built all over England. There was a great and growing demand for coal for these new factories. The trucks of coal were hauled to the port by slow, plodding horses – and a quicker method of transport was urgently needed.

Stephenson decided to construct a railway with a 'travelling engine' instead of horses to haul the trucks.

Several men had attempted to design a steam locomotive (a moving engine), based on Watt's stationary engines, but the results were disastrous. One engine overturned and nearly killed the driver; a second ran out of control and crashed into a wall; and a third blew up.

Below: The 'travelling engine' – the first locomotive – built by Stephenson to carry coal from the colliery to the port. The engine was called *Blücher*, in honour of the Prussian general who fought with Wellington at the battle of Waterloo.

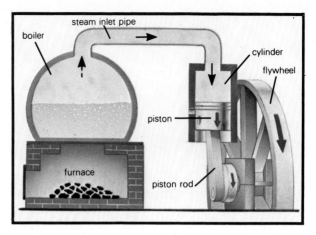

Above: An early steam engine. Steam from the boiler passes into the cylinder, so operating the piston, which in turn causes the flywheel to move round.

Below: Diagram of the stationary steam engine designed by James Watt in 1788 to pump water out of coal mines.

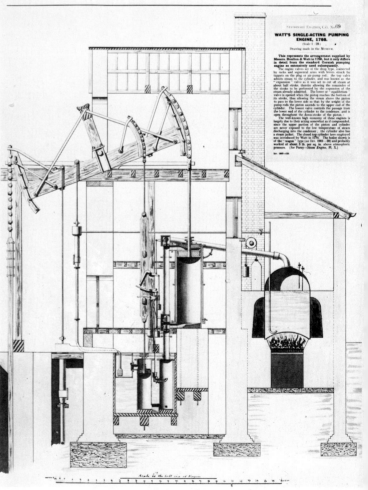

JAMES WATT 1788
SINGLE ENGINE FOR DRAINING MINES

Stephenson designed and constructed a successful locomotive. It consisted of an enormous tank with a high funnel in front, like a factory chimney, through which volumes of smoke belched out, and the front and rear wheels were linked by chains, as on a bicycle. The engine ran on metal lines and it could haul eight wagons of coal, weighing 30 tonnes, at a speed of about 7 kilometres an hour – much faster than the horses.

Delighted by the success of his colliery railway, Stephenson looked to greater things. He declared triumphantly, 'The day will soon come when people can travel by train. Railways will become the main form of transport.'

Stockton to Darlington

In 1821 Stephenson and his son Robert – now also an engineer – began to build the world's first railway to carry passengers and goods. It ran from Stockton to Darlington, with branch line to collieries, and the total distance was about 5 kilometres. The Stephensons built the railway i four years, and it was opened on 27 Septembe 1825.

Thousands of people came to watch the cere mony. They expected the engine to blow up, an they came to laugh and jeer. They were far to frightened to travel on the train.

The train, with 22 open passenger trucks and 6 goods wagons, chugged off at a speed of 8 kilometres an hour. Stephenson drove the engine and a man with a red flag rode ahead on horseback to keep the line clear.

As the engine did not blow up, spectators along the route took courage and began to scramble aboard. Soon the train was carrying over 600 passengers.

Stephenson had a good sense of fun. 'Here's

your chance, George!' he chuckled to himself. 'I'll show all these ladies and gentlemen what a steam engine can do!' He heaped on the coal and raised the speed to 20 kilometres an hour. The passengers cheered wildly.

After this momentous event, Stephenson was commissioned to build a second and more important railway, between Liverpool and Manchester. This was an immense task. It involved constructing 63 bridges and a large viaduct; hewing tunnels through rocks; and laying railway lines across about 20 square kilometres of marshland, known as Chat Moss.

The railway across Chat Moss

The decision to build this railway met with fierce opposition from the owners of canals and from farmers across whose land the railway would run. Canals then provided the main form of transport between Liverpool and Manchester and the canal companies feared that the railway would ruin their trade. The farmers protested that sparks from the engines would set fire to their crops and that the noise would stop their hens from laying eggs and their cows from producing milk.

When Stephenson and his son Robert began to survey the land, angry farmers with guns threatened to shoot them. Stephenson ignored their threats and made his survey by moonlight, when the farmers were in bed.

The survey completed, teams of workmen began to construct the bridges and hew out the tunnels. Stephenson travelled round on horseback and supervised their work, inspiring the men in his cheerful, confident manner.

Above: The nine-arch Sankey Viaduct, built to carry the Liverpool to Manchester railway across the Sankey Valley.

Below: Jointed rail, points system and signals introduced in 1842 and still used in some areas. Electric-powered signals were first used in the U.S.A., in 1884, devised by George Westinghouse. The modern system of lights was introduced in 1921.

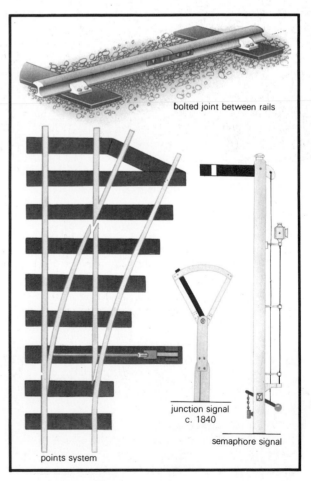

bolted joint between rails

junction signal
c. 1840

semaphore signal

points system

Stephenson performed a great engineering feat in laying the railway lines across Chat Moss. This great peat bog was over 12 metres deep, and it would not bear the weight of a man, let alone a heavily-laden train. The task seemed impossible, but Stephenson worked on the principle that whereas a man will sink in water a raft will float. He decided to lay a kind of giant raft of tree trunks and brushwood above the marshes and to build a floating railroad which, though not quite stationary, would be absolutely safe.

Load after load of tree trunks and branches was laboriously laid on the marshes to form the foundation. Gates and hurdles were placed above the trees and tons of soil and ballast were spread over the top and rammed tight. Heavy oak sleepers were pegged to this track, and the railway lines were then laid on the sleepers.

The great Duke of Wellington (then Prime Minister) opened the Liverpool–Manchester railway in September 1830, and within a few months it was carrying 1,200 passengers a day.

Stephenson's prophecy was fulfilled. During the next few years a network of railways spread like a spider's web across England, linking up the larger towns and cities – and the railways became the principal form of transport.

Stephenson, now world-famous, was asked to plan railways for foreign countries. He travelled widely and planned railway systems for several countries in Europe and for the United States of America. So the railways spread to many parts of the world.

George Stephenson – the poor boy who had no schooling – became a rich man. He died in 1848, leaving a fortune of £140,000 – a very large sum for those days.

Left: Opening of the Liverpool to Manchester railway, in 1830, by the Duke of Wellington. The ceremony ended in tragedy when the M.P. for Liverpool, William Huskisson, stepped out on to the track, and was knocked down and killed by the train.

Inset: Brushwood being laid across Chat Moss.

Below: The Metro Cammell of the 1960s (left), and the new High Speed Train, which can travel at over 200 kph, averaging 140 kph.

Louis Braille

Books for the blind 1834

Louis Braille, who was born in 1809 in the small French town of Coupvray, south-east of Paris, was the son of a saddler. A bright child, full of fun and laughter, he loved to watch his father at work.

One day, when he was three years old, Louis crept into the saddlery shop while his father was talking to a customer outside. He ran excitedly to the workbench, picked up a pruning knife and a piece of leather and tried to cut out a thong. But the leather was too tough for his small hand. The knife slipped and sprang, point first, deep into his left eye.

Louis's father heard the child's screams and rushed into the shop and removed the knife from his eye. Instead of calling a doctor, he sent for an old hermit woman who claimed to possess magic healing powers. The woman dabbed the eye with one of her concoctions, and this eased the pain and stopped the bleeding.

But the treatment was disastrous. By stopping the eye from bleeding outward, it caused it to bleed inward. Consequently the other eye also became infected. Within six months Louis Braille was totally blind.

Louis Braille is attended by the hermit woman after the accident in his father's saddlery shop.

In those days blind people were treated as a useless burden, as lunatics were at that time. Their parents often resented them, even grudging them their keep. Many poor parents sent their children to a workhouse, or sold them as freaks to a fun fair – or, worse, turned them out into the streets to fend for themselves. Homeless blind people of all ages roamed the streets of most large towns, and even well-educated men and women seemed to find it amusing to watch them groping their way and bumping into buildings. They would throw things at them or trip them up, and then burst into laughter.

Louis Braille, however, was showered with love and kindness by his family. Even so, he was very sensitive about his blindness. From being a cheerful child, he became quiet and solemn and lived in a lonely world of his own. He felt there was no future for him.

The friendly Abbé

Then, when Louis was 7, a French priest, the Abbé Palluy, put new heart into him. The kindly priest taught him about the wonders of nature, music and religion. He read him stories from the Bible with such feeling that the scenes and characters were brought to life.

'You must not think you are useless because you are blind,' the priest told Louis. 'If you try to overcome your handicap, there will be plenty of opportunities for you. Pray hard, and in time God will find you work to do.'

Above: In Braille's time, the blind were cruelly tormented by many people, who did not take the trouble to help them.

Below: The Abbé gave Louis hope and determination to overcome his handicap. He would no doubt have encouraged him with tales of famous people like the great composers, Handel and Johann Sebastian Bach, and the writer of *Paradise Lost*, John Milton, all of whom became blind during their careers.

Louis drew comfort from these words, and developed a deep, though simple, religious faith.

At the age of 10, the boy was sent to a special school for blind children in Paris – the only one in France. It was a miserable place. The building was old and dilapidated and reeking with damp. There were 60 pupils, and the headmaster treated them with great severity, punishing the boys for the most trivial offences by depriving them of their meals or sending them into solitary confinement.

At this school Louis Braille discovered his mission in life.

The blind children could not learn their lessons from books. A few books had been printed in large raised letters so that the children could feel their shape, but, as each letter was 3 millimetres tall, they took up so much space that the children often forgot the beginning of a sentence before they fingered their way to the end. The masters discarded these useless books and taught the children orally – so they had to learn their lessons by heart.

Young Braille resolved to find a way to enable the blind to read by feel. He decided to invent a special alphabet and devise a code of tiny raised signs that a blind person could immediately decipher by the sensitive tip of the finger.

He spent years experimenting with different ideas for symbols. He cut strips of his father's leather; he knocked small nails into pieces of wood; he toyed with twigs. But all his ideas were impractical.

Then Braille met an army officer, Charles Barbier, who had served with Napoleon in the Napoleonic Wars. Barbier told Braille that, by impressing dots and dashes on thin strips of cardboard, he used to issue night orders to his troops. They could decipher the orders by touch instead of flashing their torches to read.

Reading by touch
This gave Braille his clue. He thought of the game of dominoes and hit upon the brilliant idea of basing his alphabet on the six dots of the domino. With these six dots he worked out a code of 63 different combinations to cover all the letters, punctuation marks and various abbreviation signs.

Before the Braille alphabet was introduced, children were taught from books printed with raised letters. This system was introduced in 1784 by a French teacher, Valentine Haüy, who discovered that a blind pupil could 'read' a page where the script was heavily indented. He set up institutes for blind people in Paris, Liverpool and St Petersburg (Leningrad).

Braille completed his invention in 1834, when he was 25, and gave the blind the means to read.

He became a master at the school and he spent his small salary on having books printed in the dot alphabet for his pupils. The children soon learnt to read by touch – and their lives brightened. The system was so successful that Braille adapted it for writing music as well, thereby giving the children the opportunity to play the piano or any other musical instrument.

Above: A pack of Braille playing cards, against a page taken from a book printed in Braille. Today, all the best books, as well as magazines and newspapers, are available in Braille. The blind can also join 'talking book' libraries. Books are read out loud, and recorded on tapes and cassettes, which can then be played back and listened to at leisure.

Above: The early system of raised lettering took up much room, and made reading slow and arduous. With practice, the Braille alphabet was much quicker and easier to read. The system was taken up in Britain by Dr T. R. Armitage, who was himself blind. Armitage founded the Royal National Institute for the Blind in 1869.

Braille spent the rest of his life teaching the blind and helping them to overcome their handicap.

Through the damp conditions at the school, Braille developed tuberculosis. He died in 1852, two days before his forty-third birthday. His pupils felt they had lost their best friend and were deeply distressed.

At the time of Braille's death nobody outside the school knew of his wonderful invention. Sixteen years passed. Then, in 1868, it came to the notice of a blind English doctor, Dr Armitage.

Dr Armitage, quick to see the benefits of the system, immediately set up a publishing house in London and printed books in 'Braille'. Through his enterprising venture the system spread and was adopted throughout the world.

Later a method was devised to enable blind people to write in Braille – and this was followed by the invention of Braille typewriters.

Today the best books by modern authors – as well as newspapers and magazines – are published in Braille in nearly every country in the world. In Britain alone as many as 50,000 books and half a million periodicals may be printed in a single year.

The Braille alphabet, which is based upon different combinations of the six dots of a domino.

Left: A Braille typewriter. The keyboard is arranged in Braille, and the keys punch out the raised dots on the paper.

Below: Blind people work in a wide range of full-time jobs in industry, including assembly of mechanical components and electrical devices, machine and capstan lathe operating and milling. Others work as telephonists, audio and shorthand typists, and even physiotherapists and lawyers.

Thanks to Braille's invention, blind people can now take up full-time careers instead of being regarded as useless.

In 1952, the centenary of Louis Braille's death, his body was moved from its simple grave at Coupvray and buried in the Panthéon in Paris – an honour reserved for only the great.

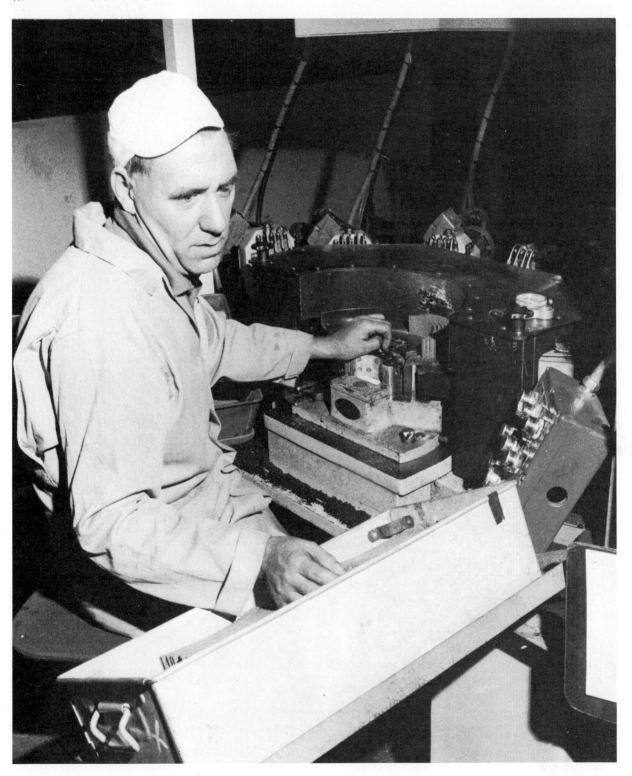

Thomas Alva Edison

The coming of electric light 1880

The nineteenth century was an age of great industrial progress. In the past everything had been made by hand. Now machines began to take the place of the slow and laborious hand methods and many forms of merchandise were mass-produced in factories.

We call this period the Industrial Revolution, and it gave great opportunities to inventors to devise machines and instruments.

One of the greatest inventors of this time was Thomas Alva Edison, an American, who was born in 1847 at Milan, Ohio. He patented more than 1,000 inventions.

Edison began to show his inventive mind at the age of 7. He set up a 'laboratory' in his parents' house and tried to make chemicals by soaking plants in jars of water. He also tried to make electric batteries out of scraps of metal and chemicals. He earned the money to buy materials for his 'experiments' by driving a horse and cart round the village and selling vegetables from his parents' garden.

Edison started his career as an inventor when he was 17. He worked for the Western Union Telegraph Company. The electric telegraph was a new system of communications and the transmitter could send only one message at a time. Edison determined to improve the system. He had no knowledge of electricity. It was only about 30 years since the British scientist Michael Faraday discovered a way to produce electricity, and few people knew anything about the subject. Edison studied Faraday's book on electricity and grasped the technicalities. After many long and difficult experiments, he invented an instrument that could transmit several messages at the same time.

Delighted with his achievement, Edison rashly gave up his job and, with only a few dollars in his pocket, went to New York to seek his fortune as an inventor.

Below: Electric telegraph. ABC transmitter (left) and ABC Wheatstone receiver (right).

Right: Edison's phonograph in use in the home.

Inset: Edison with the phonograph, which he invented in 1877. Recordings were made on a cylinder. The system of recording on discs, with the needle moving sideways instead of up and down, was invented by Emile Berliner in 1887. This machine was known as the gramophone. Early records were made of shellac, and played for about five minutes. The first 'long play' records, made of plastic, were launched in the late 1940s.

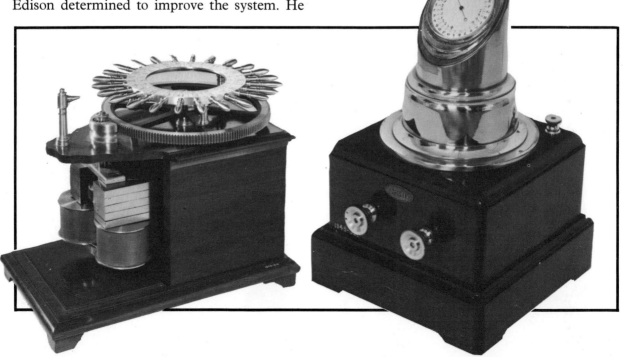

Edison's phonograph

He had the greatest good luck. He visited the Gold Indicator Telegraph Company and, while he was in the office, the transmitter broke down. It could not be repaired satisfactorily. Edison seized his opportunity. He designed a much more efficient machine, and he sold his invention to the telegraph company for 40,000 dollars.

With this money, Edison rented a small workshop and started his own business. He invented various instruments and gadgets for telegraph companies, and his business quickly grew. In 1872 he built a large factory at Menlo Park, 40 kilometres from New York, and employed about 100 men.

Edison now caused a great sensation. He invented a machine that could talk – the first gramophone.

The machine – which Edison called a 'phonograph' – consisted of a metal cylinder with a crank handle, an arm containing a blunt pin, and a speaking tube.

Edison demonstrated his phonograph to the public. He wound a sheet of tin foil round the cylinder and set the pin against the foil. He turned the crank-handle and, as the cylinder revolved, he shouted the words of the nursery rhyme *Mary Had a Little Lamb* into the speaking tube. Through the vibrations in his voice the pin made grooves in the foil and recorded his words. Edison played back the recording, and the pin ran through the grooves and repeated the rhyme.

The crowds were astonished. Many people thought Edison must be a ventriloquist. Edison proved that it was not a trick by letting some of the visitors make their own recordings.

Thousands of people bought the phonograph. There was, of course, no radio or television in those days, and they were pleased to have a new way to entertain themselves at home.

Edison was now 30 – a tall, amusing man, who smoked fat cigars and always wore shabby old clothes, with no collar or tie. He had over 120 inventions to his name and was rich and famous.

Before the advent of electric light, streets were lit by gas lamps. Gas street lighting was invented by Frederick Albert Winsor, and first used in 1814, in London.

Above left: Edison's early experiments were unsuccessful.

Edison has the idea of using carbon-coated filaments.

The first steps

In 1878 Edison began another greater venture. He decided to give the world electric light.

At that time the streets of towns, public buildings and factories were lit by dim, flickering gas lamps. Men went round the streets in the evening and lit the lamps by lighters on long poles, and in the morning they went back and turned them out again. Sometimes the gas flames blew out in a wind and a street became dark and eerie. In private houses most people used oil lamps, and every day these had to be filled and the wicks trimmed. The oil lamps often smoked and sent out clouds of soot, dirtying ceilings and walls.

Edison's first task was to make an electric light bulb. He bought some glass jars. He then tried to make a filament – the coil inside the bulb that glows and produces the light.

First he made a filament of paper with wire running through it. He put it into a glass jar and connected the ends of the wire to an electric battery. When the paper became hot, it burnt up. Edison tried several other materials, and the same thing happened. He then used a soft metal – but the metal melted.

Edison wondered if the air inside the bulb fanned the heat and made the metal too hot. So he put in a new filament and pumped the air out of the bulb. The filament glowed for ten minutes before the metal melted. This was an improvement, but Edison had to find some way to make his filaments *resist* heat and never get too hot.

He spent months trying to solve this difficult problem. He worked all day, every day, and often throughout the night; he seldom had more than three hours' sleep and sometimes he did not go to bed at all. He strained his eyes by working long hours under the dim oil lamp.

Edison made over 9,000 experiments, and they all failed. Then, quite by chance, he discovered the answer to his problem.

It was the middle of the night. Edison, alone in the silent factory, was sitting at his table in deep thought, chewing a fat cigar. His oil lamp smoked and soot fell on to the table. Edison dreamily turned his eyes – and suddenly noticed the soot. 'Carbon!' he cried. 'The filaments need a coat of carbon to resist heat.'

Next morning Edison tested this new idea. He made a filament of cotton, rolled it in soft, wet carbon, and then baked it in a very hot oven. He fitted the carbonized filament into a glass bulb, pumped out the air, and turned on the electricity.

The bulb shone brightly. The workmen cried out and gathered round Edison to watch the exciting experiment. 'How long will the light

Coated with carbon, the bulb filament stayed alight for nearly two whole days.

Above: Edison tried many filament materials before discovering a variety of bamboo which would stay alight for many months. Today, tungsten is used for bulb filaments. This is a metal with an extremely high melting point of about 3,400°C., so an intense amount of heat would need to be generated before it burnt up. The tungsten is made into a very fine wire and looped into a spiral, so that it takes up less room and can be put into the bulb more easily. Inside the bulb, the wire is supported at several points.

burn?' they wondered.

Fifteen minutes passed . . . 30 minutes . . . an hour . . . 2 hours . . . The light was still shining at the end of the day.

All through the night Edison, surrounded by his workmen, sat at his table, smoking cigars – excitedly watching the bulb and counting the hours. The long night ended and the light was still just as bright. It stayed alight for 45 hours altogether.

Edison was not satisfied. He wanted to produce a bulb with a much longer life. He experimented with several other carbonized materials. He found that bamboo fibres lasted the longest. He obtained specimens of 6,000 varieties of bamboo from different parts of the world and tested them all to see which gave the best results. He chose bamboos from the valley of the River Amazon, in South America – and produced an electric light bulb that kept alight for months.

Victory!

On New Year's Eve 1880, Edison gave an electric light display in Menlo Park to show the public his great invention. Hundreds of shining bulbs were hung in festoons from the trees and from old gas lamp posts, giving a blaze of light in the darkness. The crowds of sightseers were wild with excitement.

Above: Edison's lamps being used to illuminate a theatre in an electric light display in 1883. The picture shows the positioning of the lamps backstage. Modern theatre lighting techniques are extremely complex; often the play of light on stage is used symbolically, to add to the message of the play itself.

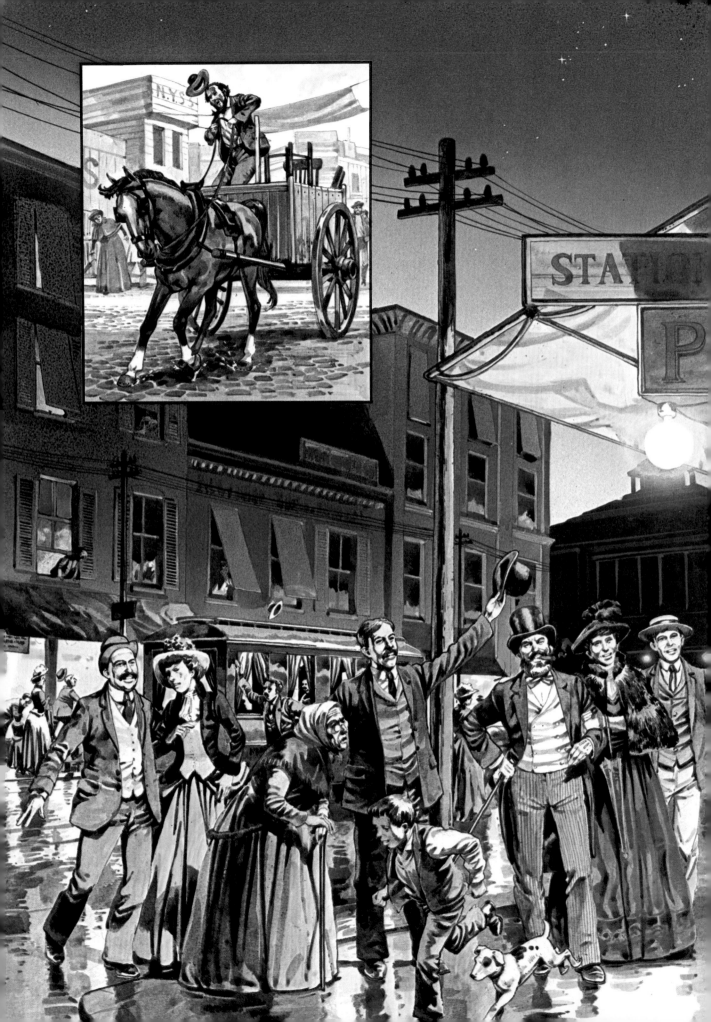

History is made

New York made history and decided to light a large district of the city by electricity – the first town in the world to use electric light.

This was an immense undertaking for Edison. He had to lay cables under about 75 kilometres of streets, wire 1,000 buildings, and build a power station to produce the electricity. He also had to invent and manufacture some 300 electrical instruments and gadgets. No factory could supply anything.

Hundreds of men dug up the streets and laid the cables, and others built the power station. When Edison turned on the electric current to test the system, horses in the streets shied and bolted! Electricity was leaking through the cables and giving the horses electric shocks. Up came the cables again for the men to repair the faults in the system.

Edison now had to get permission from the householders to wire their homes. The people were afraid that their houses might blow up and at first many refused but, after much persuasion, they unwillingly gave permission.

At last, the immense task was completed, and the great night came.

Late on the night of 4 September 1882 the lights in all the streets and buildings were put out, and the whole district was plunged into darkness. Men, women and children sat nervously in their dark houses, praying there would be no explosion; and crowds of people were gathered in the streets.

Edison entered the power station. He turned on the electric current – and all the streets and buildings burst into light.

The excitement was immense. People threw open their windows and waved and cheered, and men ran up and down the streets, throwing their hats into the air.

After this historic event countries in many parts of the world began to use electricity for light and heat; to drive machines in factories; and for many other purposes. Electricity soon became one of the world's most important industries.

On 1 August 1931 Thomas Edison died, aged 84. He had been involved in active work until just eighteen days before his death, and he had collapsed in his workshop. The last experiments he worked on were with vulcanized rubber at the Golden Rod plant.

Left: The historic light-up of New York in September 1882. Whilst Edison was working on his invention in the U.S.A., another inventor, Joseph Swan, in England experimented with a light bulb which worked on a similar principle, also with a carbon filament. This was successfully demonstrated and patented in 1878, but Swan was not able to produce it in large numbers until 1881. The two inventors formed rival companies, but eventually they joined forces under the title of the Edison and Swan United Electric Light Co. Ltd.

Inset: An electricity leak in the early days of the project caused sparks to fly from the metal in the hooves of passing horses.

Right: A special Christmas display of lights in London's Regent Street. Different themes are chosen for these displays each year. In 1979, the latest laser beam techniques were tried out.

Joseph Lister

Antiseptics: hygiene in medicine 1865

Before the middle of the last century anyone who underwent a surgical operation was in danger of losing his life because of the complete lack of hygiene in the operating theatres at hospitals.

The surgeons performed their operations on rickety wooden tables which were wedged up so that they would not topple, and a bucket of sawdust was placed underneath to catch the patient's blood. The surgeons seldom bothered to wash their hands before an operation, and they wore black morning coats, congealed with blood and dirt. The instruments were never sterilized and, indeed, were seldom even washed. After an operation, a man would wipe the instruments with a rag and toss them into a drawer in readiness for the next occasion.

An eminent surgeon of early Victorian times remarked that a person who underwent any operation was exposed to greater danger than the soldiers at the Battle of Waterloo had faced. This was probably no exaggeration. The death rate was very high. Though the majority of operations were surgically successful, more than half the patients subsequently died of blood poisoning.

The reason for the appalling, unhygienic conditions was that nobody then knew of the existence of germs.

Antisepsis

It was the French chemist Louis Pasteur who made this important discovery. During the 1850s Pasteur investigated the chemical changes that take place when grapes ferment and turn into wine. Scientists assumed that fermentation occurred automatically, but Pasteur disproved this theory. Through years of research and laboratory experiments, he discovered that microbes cause fermentation: these are germs which settle and breed on vegetable and animal matter and make it decay.

In 1865 Pasteur wrote a paper about his discovery of germs. He revealed that the air is laden with minute, invisible microbes that are carried everywhere on the dust. He expressed the opinion that these air germs might be capable of carrying disease to people.

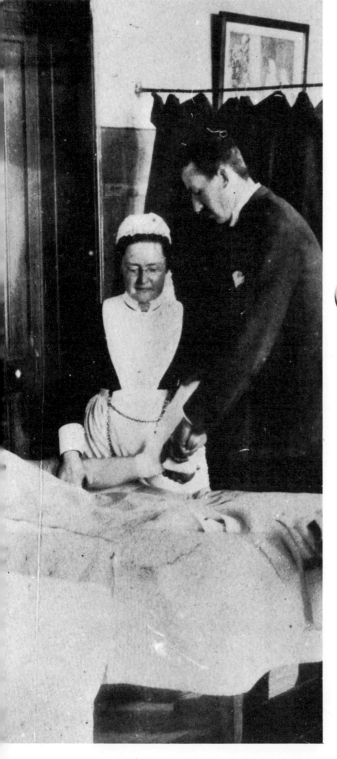

Below: A hospital in the late 1870s. Lister's portable carbolic spray, patented in 1875 and powered by a steam kettle, is being used. Carbolic sprays are no longer used, as they did not prove effective.

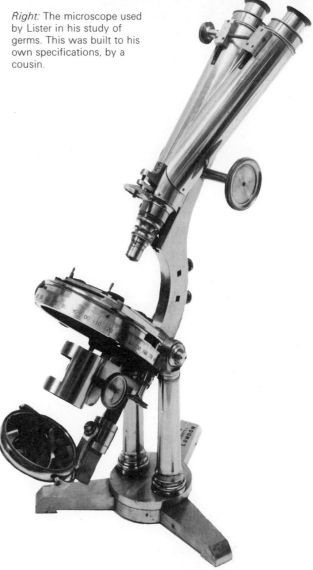

Right: The microscope used by Lister in his study of germs. This was built to his own specifications, by a cousin.

Pasteur's paper came to the notice of Joseph Lister, a brilliant young English surgeon. Like all surgeons, Lister had lost many patients from blood poisoning following operations. He had attributed their deaths to his own incompetence, and this had grieved him.

When Lister read Pasteur's report, he saw at once the medical significance of his sensational discovery. Germs in the theatre were the cause of so many deaths. The microbes settled on a patient's open wound during an operation, got into his blood-stream and poisoned him – in the same way as they destroyed vegetable or animal matter.

Lister, who was born in 1827, was now, at the age of 38, head of the surgical department of Glasgow's famous Royal Infirmary. A kind, modest man with a gentle manner, he was beloved by the doctors and nurses, who affectionately called him 'The Chief'.

31

Lister determined to devise an 'antisepsis' technique (that is, a technique to fight decay) to prevent germs in the theatre from infecting his patients during operations. He tried to produce an antiseptic chemical with the power to kill germs, but his first experiments were fruitless. He then read in a newspaper that carbolic acid was used to purify sewage.

With great daring, Lister bought a bottle of crude carbolic and tested it at an operation on a man's leg. Before the operation, Lister saturated his hands, instruments and the patient's leg with carbolic. Then, after the operation, he cleansed the wound with carbolic and dressed it with lint saturated with the disinfectant.

The vicious acid burnt the man's skin and caused him acute pain – but it killed the germs and prevented blood poisoning, and the patient survived.

By this and further successful tests Lister proved that antiseptics could prevent blood poisoning by germs. But he was dissatisfied with carbolic because of its irritation to the skin. He resumed his laboratory experiments and eventually he produced a milder but equally

Above: In an early operation at the Glasgow Royal Infirmary, Lister used crude carbolic on a man's wound. Infection was prevented, and six weeks later, the wound had healed.

Below: Some of the surgical knives used by Lister

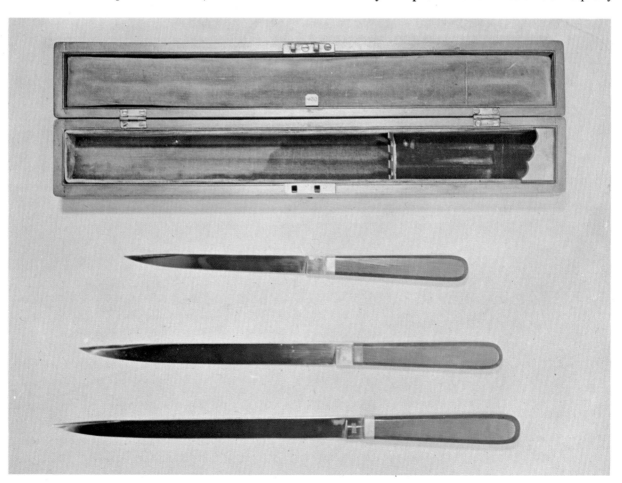

destructive antiseptic that caused the patient no
discomfort.

Asepsis

Lister now tried to destroy the germs in the
air *before* they could attack a patient. He set up a
machine and sprayed the operating theatre with
a vicious fluid that created a dense, pernicious
fog. The result was devastating. Doctors and
nurses coughed and spluttered and their eyes ran
– and Lister himself could hardly see to operate.
He soon gave up this idea.

Lister next devoted his attention to producing
an antiseptic surgical dressing. After experimenting with various materials bought from drapery
shops Lister produced a lint dressing comprising
a pad of eight layers of gauze, impregnated with
boracic acid – a dressing still widely used today.

In course of time, Lister discovered that the
risk of germs could be further reduced by heat
sterilization of surgical dressings and instruments, and also of the garments worn by the
doctors and nurses in the theatre. This new
technique, known as asepsis, brought a further
dramatic drop in the death rate.

Above: The lint dressing devised by Lister and still widely
used today. It comprises layers of gauze, which are
impregnated with boracic acid.

Below: The spray used in Lister's time to dispense carbolic
into the air during operations.

33

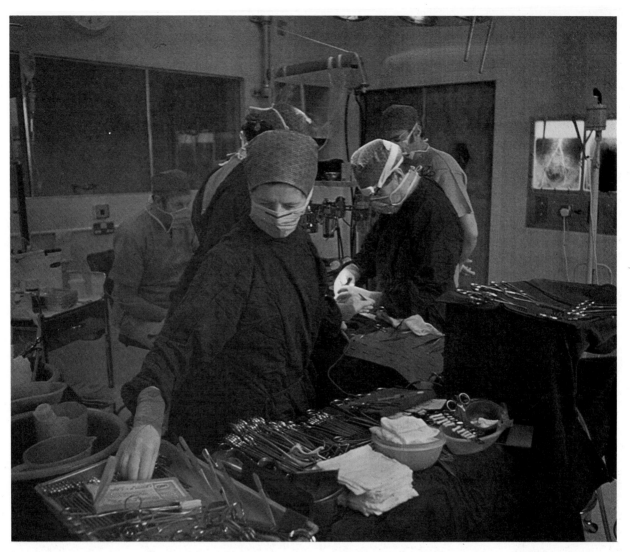

A modern operating theatre, showing the very high standard of hygiene today. Surgeons and nurses alike wear sterilized gowns, skull caps and masks, and the instruments to be used have been sterilized in preparation for the operation.

Right: The 'scrub-up room' where all medical staff scrub their hands and arms with antiseptic soap, under running water for at least five minutes. Then they put on special rubber gloves which are very fine.

Lister had won his great battle against germs. He described his techniques in a medical journal, and they aroused wide interest. Lister demonstrated his methods to surgeons from many parts of Britain, and all who watched his operations were greatly impressed. They adopted his techniques, which soon became general practice.

So Lister brought about a transformation in surgery, which, in time, spread to civilized countries throughout the world.

Today the standard of hygiene is very high. The modern operating theatre is tiled and spotless. The surgical instruments are sterilized by high-pressure steam in machines. The instruments and dressings are taken to the theatre by a sterilized passage, free of germs; and the dirty instruments and swabs are removed by a different passage so as to avoid contaminating the clean way in.

The theatre staff – surgeons and nurses – wear sterilized linen gowns, skull caps, rubber boots and masks, and before an operation they 'scrub up'. For five minutes they wash their hands and arms up to their elbows under running water with a special antiseptic soap that penetrates the pores of the skin and forms a protective film. Then they powder their hands with an antiseptic powder and put on tight-fitting sterilized rubber gloves.

As a result of these and similar precautions, the death rate is now very low.

Joseph Lister was given a peerage for his great contribution to medicine – the first doctor to receive this honour. He died in 1912, at 84.

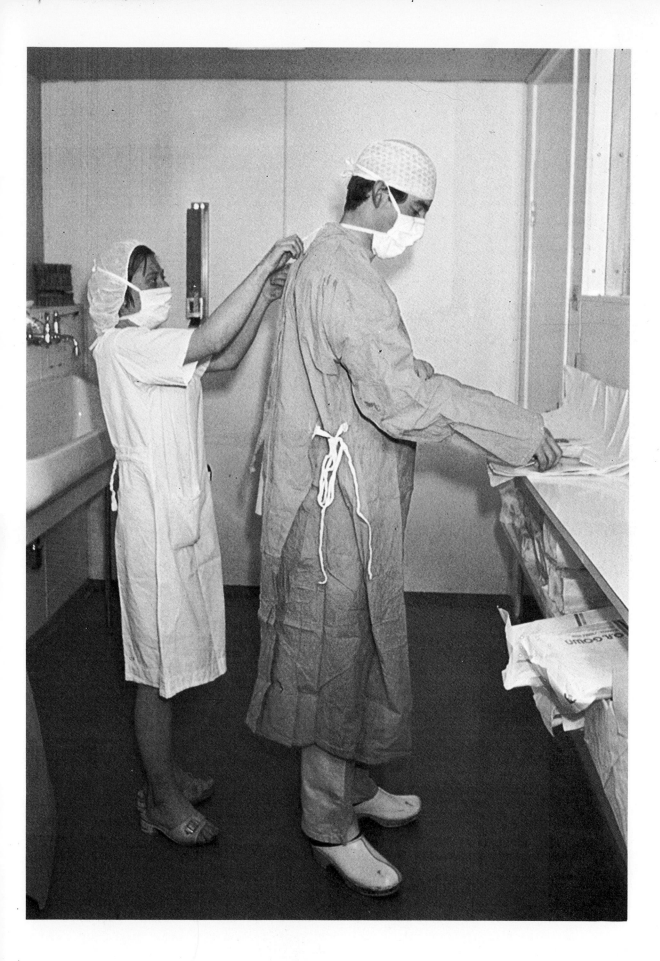

Alexander Graham Bell

The birth of the telephone 1895

The invention of the telephone was one of the greatest blessings of the Victorian age. Before that time people living even a short distance from each other had no direct means of communication. They could not have a conversation with one another when they had a question to discuss; they had to write letters and patiently wait for a reply.

Businessmen conducted their business by post and their negotiations often took a long time. When they corresponded with a firm in a foreign country across the seas their letters went by ship and several weeks might pass before they received a reply.

Urgent messages could sometimes be sent by telegraph, but the telegraph service operated only in certain districts and was very inadequate. People living in towns could hire messenger boys to deliver messages locally – but no messenger service was available in country districts.

The lack of communications often fell hard on people in the country. For example, if someone was taken ill in the night one of the family, or perhaps a servant, had to set out on horseback or on foot in the darkness and ride or trudge over fields and down muddy lanes to the nearest town to fetch the doctor. The long delay in bringing the doctor to the patient could be fatal.

Alexander Graham Bell invented the telephone. One of three brothers, he was born in Edinburgh in 1847, and his family background had a great influence on his life and work.

His father was a famous authority on elocution and had devised a system called *visible speech* for teaching pronunciation. This was a code of symbols comprising straight lines and curves which showed the position and movement of the throat, tongue and lips when pronouncing different syllables.

Canada and U.S.A.

Bell, who was very musical and had a sharp ear, took a great interest in his father's work and he showed his inventive mind at an early age by making a talking doll; he fitted a vocal gadget in the head and operated it by blowing in air with bellows. Full of fun, he played a prank with his

Left: Bell's first experiment – the 'talking doll'.

Below: Bell's career began as a teacher of deaf and dumb children. This led him to invent the first electronic hearing aid, in 1876. Early hearing aids were very cumbersome and noisy, with batteries and microphones, and it was not until the invention of the transistor in 1948 that a hearing aid which could be worn comfortably was developed.

doll in a road by a block of flats. He made the doll cry for its mother like a child in distress, and the imitation was so realistic that women rushed to comfort the child!

Bell tried to go one better and teach his dog to talk by moving its jaws and throat about – but that was too ambitious.

Following in his father's footsteps, Bell became an elocution teacher. He was then about 18 – a tall, imposing young man with thick black hair and side-whiskers and keenly intelligent eyes. As his mother had lost her hearing, Bell felt a deep sympathy for the deaf. So he broke new ground and taught deaf and dumb children to speak by his father's pronunciation code.

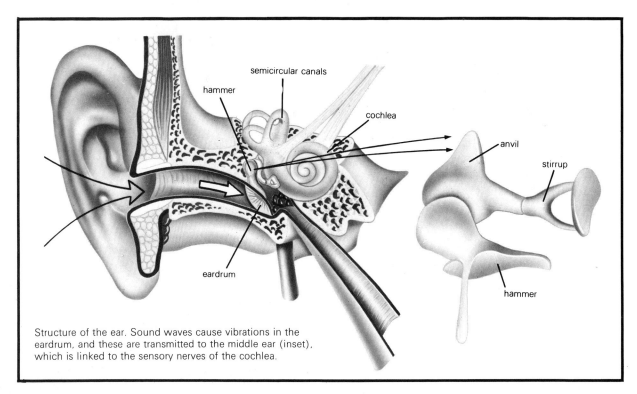

Structure of the ear. Sound waves cause vibrations in the
eardrum, and these are transmitted to the middle ear (inset),
which is linked to the sensory nerves of the cochlea.

A dedicated teacher, Bell helped numerous
children whose education would have been
neglected to overcome their speech impediment.
He was devoted to his work and his future seemed
bright. Then, in 1870, he was struck down by illness. Both his brothers had died of tuberculosis.
Now Graham (who used this name to avoid con-
fusion with his grandfather Alexander Bell, and
his father Alexander Melville Bell) contracted
the same disease. The doctors gave him only six
months to live and advised an immediate change
of climate – the only hope of saving his life.

Distraught, the family uprooted and emigrated
to Canada, settling at a place called Tutela
Heights, near the city of Brantford. Their house
overlooked the Grand River, and Bell spent his
days sitting in the shade of three tall birch trees,
enjoying the view and 'idly dreaming'. Here in
his 'thinking place', as he called it, he began to
toy with the idea of the telephone.

Before his illness, Bell had read that a German
named Helmholtz had found a way to produce
vowel sounds by means of tuning-forks, operated
by electricity. He mistakenly assumed that the
sounds were actually transmitted through a wire
– and this gave him the germ of an idea. Now,
during his long convalescence, Bell worked out a
general theory for putting the idea into practice.
'If I could make a current of electricity vary in
intensity,' he reasoned, 'I could transmit speech
by wire.'

Gradually Bell's health improved in the
Canadian air and sunshine. He went to Boston,
in the United States of America, and resumed his
work of teaching deaf and dumb children.

Now began the long and difficult experiments.
Every evening Bell shut himself in his room and
worked until the early hours of the morning,
trying to develop his theory for transmitting
speech and devise a way to generate a current of
electricity of varying intensity. He experimented
for months – but made no headway.

Then, on a sudden inspiration, Bell took his
problem to an ear specialist. The doctor gave
him a working model of a human ear. This
demonstrated the mechanism of the ear drum
and showed how the vibrations of the bones of
the inner ear give the sense of hearing.

This gave Bell his cue. He decided to devise
an electrical transmitter with a vibrating disc
that would act like a human ear drum and pick
up and relay the different sounds of speech.

Bell was not skilful with his hands and was
incapable of making such an instrument himself.
So he went to an electrical shop to enquire about
help and a mechanic named Thomas Watson
agreed to assist him.

As they worked together by night, Watson
made many different types of transmitter to
Bell's design – but all were failures. For nearly
two years they laboured in vain – and then at last
their dogged perseverance was rewarded.

Success

Bell discovered that variations in an electric current could be brought about by suspending the ends of a wire in a conducting liquid and varying its depth of suspension.

Adopting this principle, Bell designed a 'liquid transmitter', which consisted of a speaking tube and a vibrating disc with a short wire, suspended in a metal cup containing sulphuric acid and water. This cup was connected by a wire, through a battery, to a receiving instrument with a similar vibrating disc. As the speaker spoke into the tube, the vibrations in his voice vibrated the disc of the transmitter, causing the suspended wire to rise and fall in the conducting liquid and thereby vary the intensity of the electric current. The vibrations were carried along the connecting wire to the receiver – and this instrument picked up and converted the signals back to the original sounds, reproducing the words of the speaker.

On the evening of 10 March 1875, Bell and Watson tested the liquid transmitter. They set up the transmitter in Bell's bedroom and connected it by wire to a receiving apparatus in another room. Bell sat by the transmitter and prepared to make the experiment on which all his hopes were now pinned – and Watson waited at the other end of the line, holding the receiver to his ear.

Above: Bell's 'liquid transmitter' – the first stage in his invention of the telephone.

Below: Diagram of the liquid transmitter and receiver. Vibrations set up by the spoken word are carried along the connecting wire and converted back into recognizable sound by the receiver.

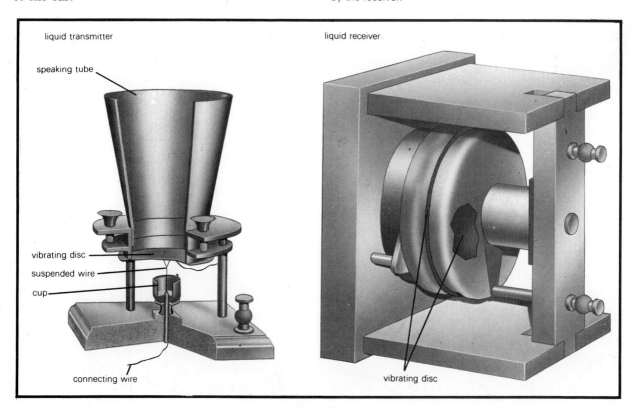

liquid transmitter

liquid receiver

speaking tube

vibrating disc

suspended wire

cup

connecting wire

vibrating disc

Tense with anxiety, Bell clumsily stretched out his arm and knocked over the battery – and the acid spilled on to his clothes. Forgetting that Watson was in a different room, he called to him for help. 'Mr Watson – come here! I want you.'

Watson heard the call through the receiver. With a cry of excitement, he ran down the passage and burst into Bell's room. 'Mr Bell!' he cried. 'I heard every word you said – distinctly!'

Victory. Bell had devised a system for transmitting speech. Now he had to see if the system would operate over a distance. He carried out some short-distance tests between houses, and all were successful. He then asked a Canadian telegraph company for permission to use their line for a long-distance test between Brantford and Paris, a town in Ontario.

The network spreads

The manager of the company did not believe that 'a piece of wire' could transmit the human voice and called Bell a black-whiskered crank. However one of his assistants, with greater foresight, persuaded the manager to allow the test.

Bell set up the transmitter in the company's office in Brantford and installed the receiver in a shoe shop in Paris, at the other end of the line. The length of the circuit, following a roundabout route, was 110 kilometres.

The test, which was witnessed by several important men, took place on the evening of 10 August 1876 – and was a crowning success. A telegraph operator telephoned from Brantford, and Bell, listening at the receiver in the shoe shop in Paris, heard the speaker's words clearly.

At the age of 29, Bell had completed his invention of the telephone. He declared triumphantly, 'The day will soon come when telephone wires will be laid to houses and friends will be able to talk with each other without leaving home.'

His prophecy soon came true. A telephone service was opened up and quickly expanded.

At first, many people were frightened of the telephone, regarding it as some kind of evil magic.

An old woman who went to a doctor's surgery· fled in terror when his wife spoke on the telephone. 'The doctor's wife has gone mad,' she told a friend. 'There was a funny kind of box on the wall with a round hole in the middle. She went to it, faced the wall and played with a handle on the box. There was a tinkle. Then she talked into the hole, pretending she was speaking to someone in the box.'

When an epidemic of smallpox broke out in Montreal, a rumour went round that the infection was being spread by people's breath being carried through the telephone wires. An angry mob with pick-axes marched on the telephone office – and soldiers were called out to disperse the rioters.

Left: The first long-distance telephone call, from Brantford to Paris (Canada). Bell listens in with Watson beside him.

Top right: In the early days, masses of telephone wires, running from the exchange to buildings, were suspended above the streets.

Right: Modern telephone exchange. 25 years after Bell's invention, one in every fifty Americans had a phone.

Far right: Evolution of the telephone. The next development seems likely to be the videophone. In the early 1970s, the Bell Telephone Company introduced the first videophone service, incorporating a television-type screen. In the future, perhaps all telephones may be linked to video-screens.

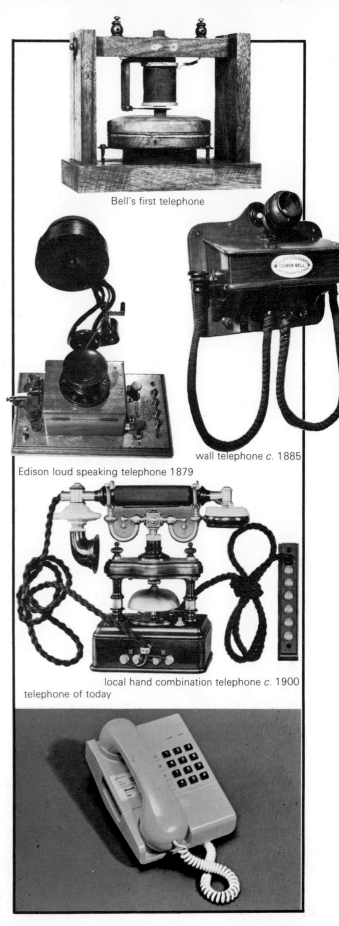

Bell's first telephone

Edison loud speaking telephone 1879

wall telephone c. 1885

Gradually the public's fears and prejudices were broken down and the telephone was acclaimed the greatest invention in the field of communications.

Bell travelled abroad and introduced his telephone to other countries – and, like a spider's web, a telephone network spread throughout the world to the benefit of many people in all walks of life.

Graham Bell died in 1922, aged 75.

local hand combination telephone c. 1900

telephone of today

Guglielmo Marconi

The early days of radio 1895

It is hard to imagine a time when there was no radio or television. Newspapers then provided the only source of news; and in the home people had to make their own entertainment in the long winter evenings, perhaps by playing games or singing songs at the piano.

Guglielmo Marconi, a young Italian from Bologna, who was born in 1874, gave the world radio. He hit upon the idea at the age of 19 during a mountaineering holiday in Switzerland.

Tired after a hard day's climbing, Marconi slumped into a chair in the lounge of his hotel and glanced at a newspaper. An article about a German physicist named Heinrich Hertz caught his eye. It reported that Hertz had discovered that magnetic waves of electricity – 'wireless' waves – travel through space at a speed of nearly 300,000 kilometres a second, the equivalent of seven times round the world in a second.

The article fired Marconi's imagination. He was for ever inventing gadgets. He believed that these wireless waves could be put to some use, and he determined to try to invent a system for transmitting messages by them.

When Marconi returned home, he began to make some experiments in the attic of his parents' luxurious Italian villa. He rigged up a makeshift transmitter and tried to send a spark from one end of a table to a metal ring at the other end. Not being a scientist, he took a long time to discover how to do this, but he persevered and eventually succeeded. He then increased the range and shot a spark the length of the attic.

Delighted by this achievement, Marconi tried a different experiment. In the middle of the night when everyone was asleep, he made the wireless waves ring an electric bell in a room two floors below the attic. Bubbling with excitement, Marconi bounded downstairs and woke up his

Below: Marconi's first laboratory was an attic room formerly used for storing silkworm trays.

Above right: Marconi's message is received. When transmitting out of the line of sight, a gun was fired to signal receipt of message.

mother to tell her his great news. He did not dare tell his father as he considered Marconi's experiments a foolish waste of time.

Further experiments

Marconi now attempted to transmit signals in Morse code. He built a more powerful transmitter and receiver and to each instrument he fitted an aerial and an earth. He connected a Morse keyboard to the transmitter and tapped out a few dots and dashes – and the receiver picked up and repeated the signals clearly.

Having thus proved that wireless waves could carry sound signals, Marconi conducted some more ambitious experiments in the garden with the help of his elder brother Alfonso. The brothers set up a receiver with an aerial on the lawn. Alfonso waited by the receiver with instructions to wave a red flag if the signals were received. Guglielmo returned to the attic and tapped out a series of Morse code dots. He gazed anxiously out of the window and, to his joy, he saw Alfonso excitedly waving the red flag.

The brothers made longer-range tests among mountains, and those were equally successful.

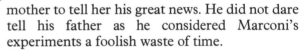

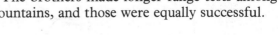

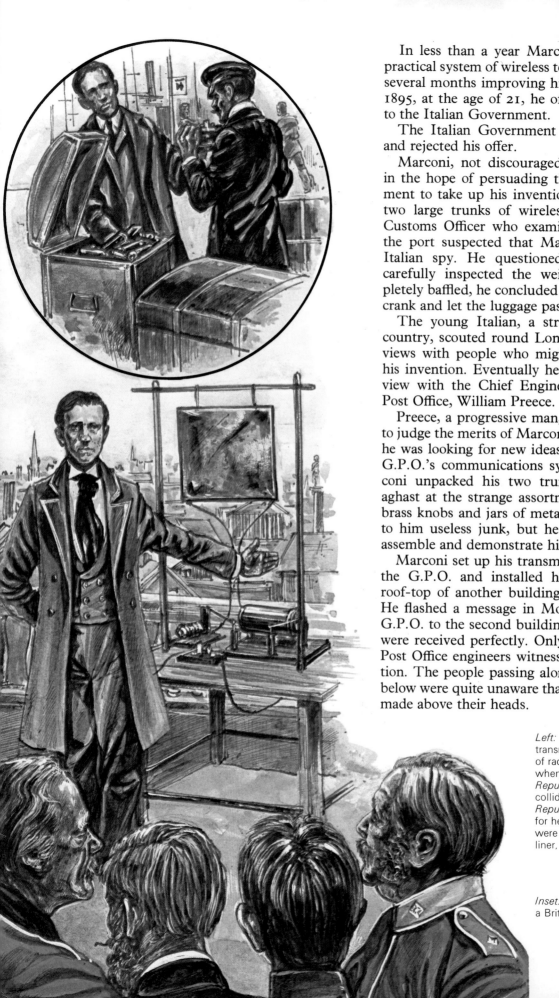

In less than a year Marconi had invented a practical system of wireless telegraphy. He spent several months improving his apparatus, and in 1895, at the age of 21, he offered his invention to the Italian Government.

The Italian Government ridiculed his ideas and rejected his offer.

Marconi, not discouraged, went to England in the hope of persuading the British Government to take up his invention. He landed with two large trunks of wireless equipment. The Customs Officer who examined his luggage at the port suspected that Marconi might be an Italian spy. He questioned him closely and carefully inspected the weird gadgets. Completely baffled, he concluded that Marconi was a crank and let the luggage pass.

The young Italian, a stranger in a foreign country, scouted round London, seeking interviews with people who might be interested in his invention. Eventually he obtained an interview with the Chief Engineer of the General Post Office, William Preece.

Preece, a progressive man, was well qualified to judge the merits of Marconi's invention – and he was looking for new ideas for improving the G.P.O.'s communications system. When Marconi unpacked his two trunks, Preece stared aghast at the strange assortment of rods, wire, brass knobs and jars of metal filings. It seemed to him useless junk, but he asked Marconi to assemble and demonstrate his apparatus.

Marconi set up his transmitter on the roof of the G.P.O. and installed his receiver on the roof-top of another building 300 metres away. He flashed a message in Morse code from the G.P.O. to the second building – and the signals were received perfectly. Only Preece and a few Post Office engineers witnessed the demonstration. The people passing along the busy streets below were quite unaware that history was being made above their heads.

Left: Marconi's rooftop transmission. The importance of radio was demonstrated when two ships, the *Republic* and the *Florida,* collided off New York. The *Republic* was able to radio for help, and 1,650 people were rescued by another liner, the *Baltic.*

Inset: Marconi is stopped by a British Customs Officer.

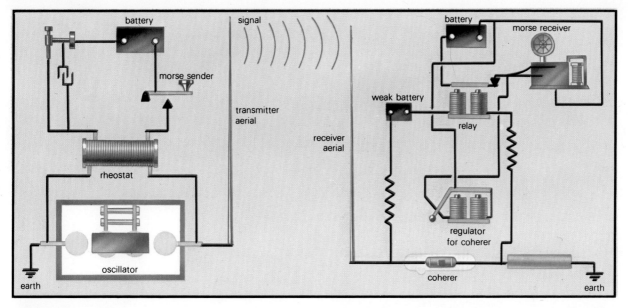

Diagram labels:
- battery
- signal
- morse sender
- transmitter aerial
- rheostat
- receiver aerial
- oscillator
- earth
- weak battery
- battery
- morse receiver
- relay
- regulator for coherer
- coherer
- earth

Official approval

Preece was greatly impressed and immediately brought Marconi's invention to the notice of the British Government. As a result, Marconi was asked to give some long-range demonstrations on Salisbury Plain to a party of government officials and army and naval officers. Marconi's whole future hung upon the success or failure of these demonstrations.

All were successful and the spectators were delighted.

The naval officers wondered if ships could send messages by wireless telegraphy instead of signalling by lamps and flags, which was then their only means of communication. They asked Marconi to give a demonstration on water.

Marconi did not know if wireless waves would cross water – but he accepted the challenge. He flashed a series of signals across the Bristol Channel – and they were received as clearly as signals on land. Marconi then crowned this achievement by sending a wireless message across the Channel, from England to France.

Later, he spanned the Atlantic and transmitted signals from Poldhu, in Cornwall, to Cape Cod in America.

Marconi's battle was won. The British Government decided to take up his invention as an aid to shipping.

Marconi built a chain of radio stations and established a wireless telegraphy service for ships in the English Channel. Soon the service was extended to other waterways. This new speedy means of communication helped to prevent many accidents at sea and greatly reduced the number of shipwrecks.

By the turn of the century all the great seafaring nations of the world were equipping their ships with radio.

Meanwhile, Marconi formed a company, opened a research laboratory and workshops at Chelmsford, in Essex, and employed a small team of scientists for the purpose of developing his invention. In course of time, he devised a system for transmitting the human voice – wireless telephony.

Above: Marconi's Morse code receiver and transmitter. The message tapped out on the morse sender is picked up by the receiver aerial.

Right: The first transatlantic wireless message, 1901. Marconi (*extreme left*) and his assistants set up the kite aerial at Cape Cod, U.S.A. The message, comprising the Morse signal for the letter S (...), was sent from Poldhu, in Cornwall.

Radio for all

The Marconi Company made and sold wireless sets with headphones, and on 23 February 1920 they gave their first public broadcast. The programme was very dull, consisting of a news bulletin and some indifferent music – but the listeners were greatly excited.

The broadcast caused such a sensation that many people made their own wireless sets to listen to future programmes. This was quite simple. A wire was wound round a tube of cardboard, and a piece of mineral, known as a 'crystal', was attached to one end of the wire. A fine metal thread, called a 'cat's whisker', rested on the crystal and was connected through headphones to the other end of the wire. A tuning condenser was made of an old tin; the set was earthed by a wire to a water pipe; and an aerial wire was hitched to a tree in the garden. The home-made crystal sets crackled and squeaked and reception was appalling but, no matter, people enjoyed listening to the broadcasts.

To meet the growing demand, six companies, headed by Marconi's firm, were now manufacturing wireless sets. In 1922 they joined forces and formed the British Broadcasting Company – the now famous BBC – and began to broadcast regular programmes in the evenings.

Their first studio was a miserable little room above a shop in London, and the walls were draped with net curtains to reduce the echoes. One evening the curtains caught fire in the middle of a programme, and the studio staff ripped them off the walls and flung them out of the window into the street. On another occasion a singer had to stand on a pile of books to reach the microphone; he took a step back on a high note and fell to the floor.

From this shaky start, the standard of broadcasting rapidly improved. The BBC set the lead, and in a few years broadcasting stations were established in many other countries. Soon a radio network linked the world, providing a speedy system of communications and a new form of entertainment for the home, brightening the lives of people everywhere.

Marconi was awarded the Nobel Prize for his great work. King George V knighted him, and the Italians who had so disdainfully rejected his invention showered Marconi with honours and treated him almost like royalty.

Marconi died in Italy of a sudden heart attack in 1937 – and the news of his death was announced to the world by radio.

Far left: A cat's whisker radio set can be built from pieces of junk.

Top left: A homemade wireless crystal set, with headphones, in use. These were relatively inexpensive and simple to construct.

Above: The first mobile outside broadcast unit, in 1919 – a bus equipped with radio for what was then known as 'wireless telephoning'.

Right: Disc jockey Kenny Everett broadcasts on the radio. There is now a network of local commercial radio stations, covering the whole of Britain.

Marie Curie

Radiotherapy to treat disease 1898

As a child Marie Curie used to gaze in wonderment at her father's scientific instruments and have childish dreams of becoming a scientist herself. Her dreams came true. She became the world's first great woman scientist, and with her husband Pierre she discovered radium – a great milestone in the battle against disease.

Marie Curie was a Pole; she was born in Warsaw in 1867 and her maiden name was Sklodovska.

She had a great struggle to obtain a scientific training, and her sister, Bronya, who wanted to be a doctor, had the same difficulty. The girls could not study at Warsaw University because women students were not admitted. The only university open to them was the Sorbonne, in Paris – but their father, a science master, could not afford to send them to the Sorbonne.

The only way for the girls to achieve their ambitions was to pay for their training themselves. So the devoted sisters made a pact to help each other. Bronya had saved enough money to pay her expenses for one year, and so she went to the Sorbonne first. Marie obtained a job as a governess, and she sent part of her salary to Bronya and saved the rest for her own training. After six long years Bronya qualified as a doctor and her struggles ended. Now it was her turn to help Marie.

Marie, who was now 24, went to the Sorbonne with a determination to excel. Brilliantly clever, she aimed to gain first class degrees in two subjects, physics and mathematics, and she devoted herself to her studies with immense enthusiasm.

For a few months Marie lived with Bronya, who was now married to a doctor. Bronya and her husband, Casimir, often took Marie to the theatre or a dance in the evening, or else they might entertain friends at home. Marie, who by nature was full of life, enjoyed these social evenings, but she felt that she ought to be studying instead of idling away her time in pleasure.

Regretfully, Marie left her sister's home and went to cheap lodgings – a miserable little room in an attic that was bitterly cold in winter and

Above: The Sorbonne (University of Paris), where Marie Curie gained her degrees in mathematics and physics. The Sorbonne was founded in 1257 by the chaplain of Louis IX. Originally a technical college, it became a university in 1808.

Below: Marie Curie.

stifling hot in summer. Every evening after a
hard day's work at the Sorbonne Marie sat in
her bleak room and spent hours studying
scientific books. She could not afford to heat the
room, and shivered with cold in the winter
evenings. She had not enough money even to
feed herself properly; she lived on bread and
butter, fruit, chocolate and an occasional egg.

Marie became weak and exhausted. One
evening when a friend called to see her she
fainted. The friend fetched Casimir. He was
shocked by Marie's condition and took her
straight back to his flat; and Bronya fed and
nursed her. As soon as Marie regained her
strength, she returned to her miserable lodgings
and worked with the same tenacity.

Marie achieved her target and gained two
first class degrees, coming top in physics and
second in mathematics.

A remarkable partnership

In 1895 Marie married Pierre Curie, a teacher
of physics and chemistry, who was about nine
years older than herself. They formed the most
remarkable partnership in the history of science.

Marie wanted to become a Doctor of Physical
Science, and to achieve this she had to carry out
some original research and write a thesis on the
result. She was trying to find a subject for her
researches, when she read a report by a French
scientist named Henri Becquerel, who was
conducting some experiments in heat radiation.
During one of his experiments, Becquerel laid a
piece of uranium on a sealed box of photographic
plates. When he opened the box, he found to his
astonishment that the plates were fogged, as if
they had been exposed to the light. As it was
impossible for light to reach them, Becquerel
concluded that the uranium emitted rays which
had penetrated the box and caused the fogging
of the plates.

Marie Curie studied under Henri Becquerel, who won the
Nobel Prize in 1903 for his discovery of the natural radioactivity in uranium. The investigation of this was left to Marie,
who continued his researches.

Marie and Pierre worked together to analyse the elements in pitchblende. In 1898 they succeeded in isolating polonium and discovered radium. It was not until 1910, four years after Pierre's death, that Marie achieved the isolation of radium. She was at that time holder of the chair of physics at the Sorbonne. Her work was carried on by her daughter, Irène, who, assisted by her husband, Jean Frédéric Joliot, discovered artificial radioactivity in 1931.

Fascinated by Becquerel's experience, Marie Curie decided to investigate radioactivity – an exciting new field for research.

Marie had no laboratory; she worked in a cold, dilapidated shed with a skylight window and a leaky roof. She made some experiments with uranium and discovered that this element emits energy rays into the air. From this she deduced that radioactivity is concerned with atoms: atoms break up and send out electrically charged particles. This was a very important discovery.

Marie's next excitement came when she tested some pitchblende, a mineral containing uranium. To her astonishment, she found that the radioactivity of pitchblende was far greater than the small percentage of uranium in the mineral could account for. The pitchblende must also contain some other radioactive element – an element unknown to scientists.

Marie Curie now enlisted the help of her husband Pierre, and together they endeavoured to discover this mysterious element. Marie systematically separated every substance of which the pitchblende was composed, and Pierre then tested each substance for radioactivity. They found that the mineral contained *two* unknown radioactive elements. They called

the first 'polonium' after Marie's native Poland, and they named the second and more important element 'radium', from the Latin word *radius*, which means ray.

The Curies needed tonnes of pitchblende to extract the radium. (Six tonnes produces only one gram.) They could not afford to buy the expensive mineral, but, through a friend, they obtained the ore free of charge from some mines in Austria.

Marie and Pierre carried out numerous chemical experiments for extracting the radium. 'I sometimes passed the whole day stirring a boiling mass of pitchblende with a rod nearly as big as myself. It was killing work.' Marie later recalled.

The Curies toiled for four years. Then, in 1902, they achieved success.

Success and tragedy

They now had a daughter, Irène, and one evening after putting her to bed they had a sudden impulse to return to their workshop. They opened the door – and in the darkness they saw a pale blue luminous glow coming from a glass container on a shelf. It was the glow of radium. They were speechless with excitement.

Pierre and Marie discover that radium glows in the dark. Radium rays are so powerful that they can penetrate most substances, causing them, and the radium itself, to fluoresce.

A lump of pitchblende.

The rays present in pitchblende were powerful enough to fog a photographic plate.

The Curies tested the radium and found that its rays were so powerful that they could penetrate almost any substance. Pierre wondered if radium might have a medical value. He exposed his arm to the rays, and they made a deep wound in his skin. He then made some tests on diseased animals – and the powerful rays healed their wounds.

Pierre expressed the belief that radium could cure diseased cells in the human body and destroy tumours in some forms of cancer – and his theory proved correct.

The Curies could have made a fortune if they had patented their process for producing radium but, poor as they were, they did not wish to take personal advantage of their discovery. They revealed their secrets to the world in the interests of humanity, and a method was devised for treating cancer patients with radium.

In 1903 Marie and Pierre were jointly awarded the Nobel prize for physics for their great work.

Three years later their brilliant partnership ended in tragedy. Pierre was knocked down in a street by a wagon and horses, and was killed.

Marie was heartbroken. She immersed herself in her work and conducted extensive researches into the use of radium for medical purposes. In 1911 she again won the Nobel prize, this time for chemistry, and became the first person to receive this high honour twice.

In 1914 an Institute of Radium was established in Paris for the study of radioactivity and the development of radiotherapy for the treatment of disease. Marie Curie was in charge of the radioactivity section. Her daughter Irène, who

Above: Pierre Curie receives the Davy Medal in November 1903 for the discovery of radium. Pierre had to accept the medal on Marie's behalf as well, as the laws of the Society at the time prevented women from attending this meeting.

Right: An X-ray of radium being used in the treatment of cancer.

was now also a scientist, assisted Marie in her experiments; and together they trained technicians in radiology.

Marie Curie continued with her work until two months before her death. Through her constant exposure to the rays of radium, her bone marrow was destroyed – and she died, the victim of her own discovery, at the age of 66, in 1934.

After her death, Irène carried on her mother's work with outstanding success – and later she also won the Nobel prize for chemistry.

Exposure to radium rays could destroy animal tissues, and cause deep burns.

Radium proved effective in healing the tumours of diseased animals. The main difficulty was to produce enough radiation to destroy the tumour, without damaging healthy cells.

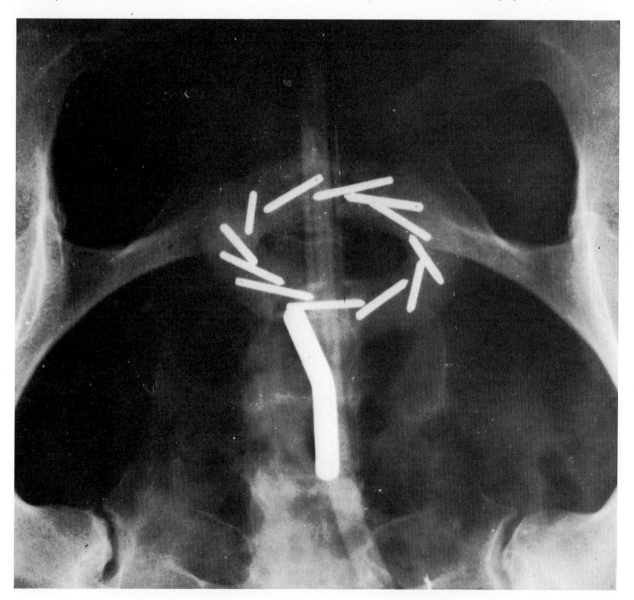

Wilbur and Orville Wright

Conquest of the air 1903

From time immemorial it had been the dream of man to fly. Men put on artificial wings and tried to fly like birds. One daredevil, wearing wings composed of birds' feathers, 'took off' from the walls of a castle, and fell into the moat and broke his leg. He was lucky. Many men killed themselves. Eventually it came to be realized that it was not possible for a man to fly like a bird because he has not sufficient muscular strength.

In the sixteenth century the great Italian painter Leonardo da Vinci designed a flying machine in imitation of a bird, with flapping wings operated by pulleys and levers. Though nothing came of his invention, Leonardo put forward some notable theories concerning the problems of flight.

For nearly 200 years scientists tried to devise a way to conquer the air. In 1783 two Frenchmen – the Montgolfier brothers – sent the first men into the sky in a balloon filled with hot air. A further 100 years passed. Then in 1896 a German named Otto Lilienthal built a glider and made a series of short glides, lasting a few seconds, down the side of a hill.

Lilienthal's daring escapades led to the invention of the aeroplane by two young Americans, Wilbur and Orville Wright.

Left: Early attempts to fly, by imitating birds and making artificial wings, and jumping off tall buildings, all ended in disaster.

The legend of Icarus, the earliest flyer, tells how he constructed a pair of wings made of feathers, held together with wax. He became too ambitious and flew too near the sun. The wax melted and he plunged to his death in the Aegean Sea.

Right: A cardboard box flung across the room gave Wilbur Wright the idea of 'warping' the wings of a glider. This, combined with a rudder, gave the pilot a much greater degree of control over the direction of the glider.

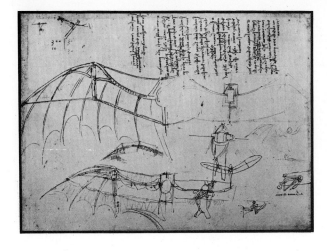

Wing warping

The Wright brothers, who were in their twenties, ran a bicycle shop at Dayton, Ohio. They were bored with making bicycles and were looking for some more interesting form of engineering. One day when business was slack, they scanned a newspaper for some ideas. They read an account of Lilienthal's gliding experiments and were enthralled.

The enterprising young brothers decided to improve upon the glider and construct a machine that could fly by mechanical power – an aeroplane driven by an engine.

They studied reports of all the various theories and previous experiments and saw that one vitally important factor had been disregarded: the effects of air-pressure on a machine in flight. A glider stayed in the air for only a few seconds because its wings did not offer sufficient resistance to the wind; consequently it toppled over, lost height and came down.

The Wrights had to devise a way to control the wings so as to resist the wind and maintain the balance of their aeroplane. This was essential for sustained flight.

Wilbur found the answer to this problem by chance while serving a customer with a tube for a bicycle tyre. He twisted, or 'warped', the cardboard box in which the tube had been packed so

Above left: Leonardo da Vinci (1452–1519) was many hundreds of years ahead of his time with his sketch of a 'flying machine'. He annotated his drawings in a left-handed right to left script.

Above: The Wright brothers' bicycle shop at Dayton, Ohio. Wilbur Wright is in the centre.

that one side pointed upwards and the other downwards. He tossed the box into the air – and it glided on a straight course down the shop.

The brothers tried out this idea with a kite. They fixed long cords to the wings and sent the kite into the sky. By pulling one cord tight and slackening the other, they warped the wings to different angles according to the wind. The kite kept on an even keel and also rose to a greater height. Encouraged by the success of this experiment, the Wrights built a glider on the same principle and glided above a beach. They found they could warp the wings and balance the glider in flight just as easily as they had controlled the kite from the ground.

Wilbur and Orville spent the next two years studying technicalities. They compiled an air-pressure table. Then they made 200 models of aeroplane wings of different shapes and sizes, tested each one in a wind tunnel, and plotted the results on a graph. They also made more than 1,000 glides in different weather conditions. Through their numerous experiments, they gradually mastered the main technical problems of flight.

In 1903 the Wrights built the world's first aeroplane. It had two wings of about 12 metres span, twin propellers, and an elevator tail that moved like a rudder. A 12 horse-power engine was mounted on the lower wing, and it was linked to the propeller shafts by bicycle chains to provide the 'drive'.

On a bitterly cold morning in December the brothers hauled their aeroplane to the lonely, windswept sands of Kitty Hawk, on the coast of North Carolina, for a trial flight.

Orville, who was pilot, clambered aboard and lay precariously on his stomach between the wings. He released a wire that was anchoring the machine to the sands and grabbed two control sticks – one to operate the elevator, which controls the aircraft's rate of climb, and the other to warp the wings. Slowly the plane bumped forward – and Wilbur ran beside it, gripping one wing to keep it steady. The machine rose about three metres into the air – and then dived to the ground. The flight lasted 12 seconds. The brothers, taking turns in piloting, then made three more, slightly longer, flights.

Delighted by their achievements, they returned to their hut on the sands, shivering with cold, and cooked themselves a hot meal. Then they sent a telegram to their father, reporting their triumphs. *Success! Four flights against wind with engine power alone. Average speed through air 31 miles* (50 km) *an hour. Longest flight 59 seconds. Inform Press.*

The Press did not believe their claim to have built and flown an aeroplane. It seemed too fantastic, and they refused to report the event.

The Wright brothers prepare to take off on their historic first powered controlled flight on 17 December 1903. Their biplane, the *Flyer*, is now housed in the National Air Museum (Smithsonian Institution) in Washington D.C., in the U.S.A.

Public acclaim

The venturesome young men now rented a field, built a workshop and hangar, and spent three years designing, constructing and testing more powerful aeroplanes. People living near their airfield watched their flights in wonderment, amusement – and awe. They feared that the young daredevils would kill themselves, and whenever their plane began to descend for its bumpy landing men and women would rush across the field with first-aid equipment and stand-by to rescue them.

Wilbur and Orville made nearly 400 flights without any serious mishap. With each new machine they overcame faults and improved the design – and gradually they increased the period of their flights from seconds to minutes and their distances from metres to kilometres, and they also climbed to greater heights. On their longest flight they encircled their airfield for 38 minutes and covered a distance of 34 kilometres; finally they were forced to land because they had run out of fuel.

After this sensational performance, the Wrights at last commanded attention and respect. The newspapers now hailed their aeroplane as the greatest invention of the age and, after this blaze of publicity, people travelled from far and wide to watch their flights.

The brothers built an aeroplane with an open cockpit to seat two passengers and they gave 'joy rides' for sightseers who were brave enough to risk their lives. Most of the passengers were terrified – and were relieved when the plane landed safely.

In 1908 the American and French governments invited the Wright brothers to give public flying demonstrations in their countries. This was their great opportunity, and they were filled with glee.

Orville gave the demonstrations in America. He made a series of successful solo flights, his longest flying time being one and a quarter hours. He also took up passengers. Unhappily, his last passenger flight ended in disaster: a propeller blade cracked and Orville lost control of the

Many people flocked to watch the early flights.

Inset: Spectators were given the chance to be among the first air-borne passengers. The very first person to fly in a glider was the coachman of Sir George Cayley. He was sent on a flight over the Yorkshire Dales in 1853, but he had no means of controlling the glider, and soon crash-landed.

machine; the plane crashed, the passenger was killed, and Orville suffered a permanent injury to his hip. But in spite of this accident, the Americans were greatly impressed.

Meanwhile, Wilbur gave a flying display in France and won even greater glory by making a sustained flight of two hours and twenty minutes. As Wilbur stepped out of his plane, a crowd of men and women, delirious with excitement, rushed forward to embrace him. 'This man has conquered the air!' the French newspapers proclaimed.

Government contracts

Triumph! The governments of both America and France gave the Wrights contracts to build aeroplanes.

Wilbur and Orville built an aircraft factory and a flying school at Dayton and went into production on a large scale in America. Later, companies were formed in France, Germany and Britain for the manufacture of aeroplanes under licence.

The aircraft industry was born.

Many great deeds of daring were performed by the pioneers who flew the aeroplanes in the early days.

The first historic event was a race for a prize of £1,000 for the first man to fly across the Channel, from Calais to Dover. Only two men were brave enough to compete – a Frenchman, Louis Blériot, and an Englishman, Hubert Latham. Latham took off first but his engine failed and his machine dived into the sea; the Englishman sat on the wreckage, coolly smoking a cigarette, and was rescued by a French ship. Before he could make a second attempt, Blériot outwitted him by making his flight during the night. The Frenchman was caught in a thick mist over the Channel; he could see nothing, and, having no instruments to guide him, he lost all sense of direction. Suddenly the great white cliffs of Dover loomed out of the mist. Narrowly missing the cliffs, Blériot made a perilous landing in a field – and won the prize.

In 1919 Alcock and Brown made the first non-stop flight across the Atlantic, from Newfoundland to Ireland. In a plane that was far from safe, they flew blind through fog nearly the whole way – and finally landed in a bog.

One of the greatest pioneers was a woman – Amy Johnson, a typist from Yorkshire. She flew solo from England to Australia in 19 days. A year later she made a return flight to Japan, crossing bleak Siberia. She then crowned her achievements by flying to the Cape and back in record times.

During the 1920s the first airliners were built, and airline companies in America, France, Germany and Britain began to operate air transport services for passengers and cargo.

Alan Cobham, a young British airman, made a series of daring flights to chart routes across the world and find suitable landing places for the airliners. On each flight, he made a detailed survey of air currents and storm tracks, noted the reactions of his aircraft to changes in temperature and climate, and made a comprehensive geographical survey of each route.

The age of air travel was dawning.

Wilbur Wright died in 1912, but his brother Orville lived to see these great developments – and he made a fortune from the aeroplane. He died in 1948, aged 76.

Right: The world's first supersonic airliner, *Concorde.* A joint Anglo-French project, *Concorde* flies at a height of over 18,000 m and reaches speeds of over 2,000 kph.

Top left: Amy Johnson, the English typist who gave up her job to become one of the great pioneers of aviation. She made historic solo flights to Japan, Australia and Africa. She was killed in 1941 when her transport aircraft crashed.

Top right: Alcock and Brown who, in 1919, made the first flight across the Atlantic, from Newfoundland to Ireland, in a plane which had no guiding instruments.

John Logie Baird

The start of television 1925

John Logie Baird, one of the pioneers of television, was always short of money and struggling to make ends meet. Casual in his behaviour, he wore shabby clothes, was generally slovenly in his appearance, and seemed to have little or no ambition.

The son of a Scottish minister, Baird, who was born in 1888, went to three schools and disliked them all. He gained a science degree and obtained an engineering post with an electricity company at a miserable salary of thirty shillings (£1.50) a week. He hated the job and gave it up when he was only 26 – and that was the end of his 'career'.

Baird wanted to be his own master and earn his living in a leisurely way. He was full of bright ideas. He tried to manufacture artificial diamonds by electrically exploding carbon rods in buckets of concrete: there was a tremendous explosion and he nearly blew up the electricity power station. Baird then had another 'brainwave'. He suffered from cold feet so he invented a kind of thermostatic sock to keep the feet warm in winter and cool in summer. With only £10 in the bank, he manufactured and sold his patent socks to some shops in Glasgow. He earned just enough money to keep himself, but he soon had to give up the business because his health broke down.

Baird emigrated to Trinidad, hoping that the hot, sunny climate might improve his health. He started a jam factory in a hut – but nobody bought his jam. Baird returned home in disgust and tried to scratch a living by selling fertilisers and soap – but he soon grew tired of that tedious job. A better idea came to him. He invented pneumatic soles for shoes – but when he tested a pair the soles burst, and so they were a failure.

Baird wasted nearly ten years of his life drifting from one crazy idea to another in the hope of making his fortune. He had no income and was now almost penniless. Then, at the age of 35, he had a great inspiration.

Pictures by wireless waves

It was 1923 – the year after the B.B.C. was founded – and Baird was staying with an old school friend at Hastings, in Sussex. One day while walking along the cliffs, his thoughts turned to radio and the broadcasts by the B.B.C. Suddenly he conceived the idea of 'seeing by wireless'. During his walk, Baird worked out in his head a detailed system for transmitting pictures by wireless waves – *television*.

Television functions on the same principle as sound radio but the process of transmitting pictures is much more complicated. Today, highly scientific electronic equipment is used.

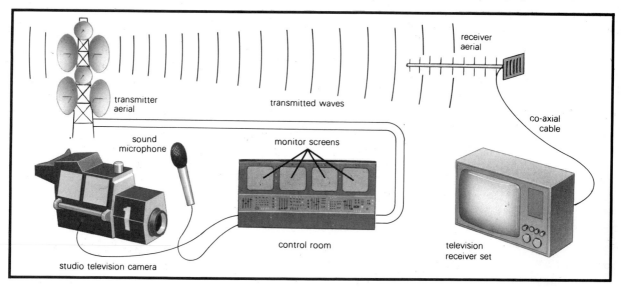

An electron beam in the camera 'scans' the image (the subject televised) in lines from left to right, as one reads a page of a book, and breaks down the picture into thousands of spots of light of different degrees of brightness. These light signals, called 'electrical impulses', shoot through space on a wireless wave and are picked up by a receiver. Another electron beam in a cathode ray tube in the television set then scans a luminous coating on the back of the tube – and the pictures appear on the screen.

Baird's system was elementary by comparison with the electronic techniques of today. He had no money to buy expensive equipment and had to make do with any odds and ends he could lay his hands on. He scratched around scrap yards and unearthed some radio valves, an old electric fan-motor, a bicycle lamp, an obsolete wireless telegraphy transmitter, and other junk. He begged a tea chest and a biscuit tin from a grocer, a hat box from a milliner, and some knitting needles from a haberdasher.

With glue, sealing wax and string, Baird rigged up a clumsy apparatus in his bedroom at his friend's house – and put his ideas to the test. He made a revolving scanner by cutting a cardboard disc from the hat box and punching holes round the edge, and he fixed the disc on the spindle of his old fan-motor. Then he placed a cardboard cross in a pool of electric light in front of the scanner, and started up his motor. As the scanner revolved, a flickering shadow of the cross was transmitted on to a white sheet behind.

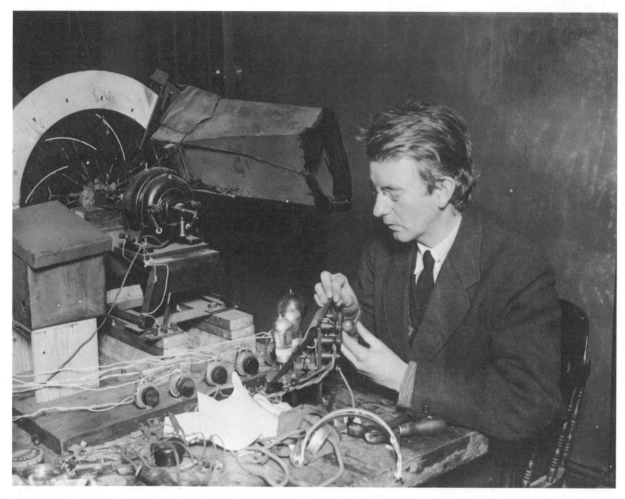

This simple experiment with junky apparatus proved that Baird's ideas were practical. He now had to find some money to buy better equipment and extend his experiments. Baird brazenly wrote letters to the newspapers telling of his invention, and appealed to readers for assistance. A wireless dealer gave him £200 in return for a share in his invention – a bad bargain for Baird, but he needed the money desperately.

Baird rented a room in Hastings, bought some good new equipment and constructed a more powerful apparatus. Working by day and by night, he spent many weeks experimenting, and gradually began to achieve better results.

Then, through carelessness, Baird had an accident that might have cost him his life. He connected several hundred batteries together, amounting to about 2,000 volts. Absent-mindedly, he put his hands on the two ends of the circuit – and nearly electrocuted himself. The landlord feared that Baird might blow up his house by his 'mad experiments' and ordered him to leave.

A worried lady

Baird went to London and lodged in an attic of an office building in Soho. He ran out of money again – and this time he could find no one to help him out. Then one day he received an unexpected visit from Gordon Selfridge, head of the famous London store. Selfridge had heard about Baird's invention and he engaged Baird to give daily demonstrations at his store for a fee of £25 a week.

The shoppers were fascinated by the demonstrations – but some were also alarmed. They were afraid that the television camera might penetrate walls and see into their homes and expose their private lives. One lady feared that she might be photographed in her bath. 'Will I be safe if I draw the curtains?' she asked Baird.

The demonstrations were very crude, but they gave Baird valuable publicity – and brought in money. Baird made further technical improvements, and on 2 October 1925 he achieved his first goal. He televised a ventriloquist's dummy and transmitted a picture of the dummy's facial features, instead of just a blurry shadow.

With a cry of excitement, Baird ran downstairs, only half-dressed, to find a real person to televise. He seized a frightened office boy, William Taynton, and set him front of the camera. He switched on the apparatus and, as the scanner revolved, the face of young Taynton appeared on the small television screen – the first person in the world to be televised.

Baird followed up his triumph by giving a successful television demonstration in public. The newspapers reported the event with glowing praise – and Baird immediately became world-famous. He received many offers of money to develop his invention, and his financial struggles were ended.

Baird formed a company and opened workshops and laboratories. With the assistance of a team of engineers and scientists, he spent three years improving his system, gradually extending the range of transmission and bettering the quality of the pictures.

Left: Baird adjusts the transmitter of one of his later sets, built in 1925.

Below: Baird's first successful transmission; the face of office boy William Taynton appears on the screen.

Baird badgered the BBC to take up his invention, and on 30 September 1929 they reluctantly staged an experimental television broadcast. The programme was very dull – two men discussing some boring subject. As there were no separate channels for sound and vision, they spoke into the microphone first and then turned and silently faced the camera with self-conscious grins, as if they were advertising some toothpaste.

Like sound radio, television started very shakily. The performers were so heavily made up that they looked like circus clowns. They were almost overcome by the heat and blinded by the fierce lights. One famous man who faced the camera for an interview shaded his eyes with his hand and exclaimed: 'The light's dazzling me! I can't think!' He swung round and turned his back to the camera.

A cruel blow

During this period of experimental television broadcasting, Baird suffered a cruel blow. His system, with the revolving scanner, was an entirely mechanical process and its scope was therefore limited; it was not possible to transmit pictures of very sharp definition. Two British firms, the Marconi Company and Electrical Musical Instruments (E.M.I.), working together, devised a greatly superior electronic television

system, capable of transmitting much sharper pictures.

In 1937 a committee tested and compared the two systems. The BBC decided to adopt the Marconi–E.M.I. system – and poor Baird, the pioneer, was eclipsed. He died nine years later, a broken man.

Television made little progress until after the Second World War (1939–45). The highlight came with the Coronation of Queen Elizabeth II, on 2 June 1953.

The BBC televised the great pageant in all its splendour – the processions to Westminster Abbey of the royal family, foreign kings and queens, heads of state and other dignitaries; the great assembly inside the Abbey; the crowning of the Queen; and, finally, her return to Buckingham Palace in a glass coach, wearing her robes and crown and holding the sceptre.

About 20,000,000 people watched the ceremony on television. Viewing parties were held in private houses and thousands of people bought tickets and watched the event on television screens set up in hotels, cinemas, shops, offices and other public places.

Most of the viewers had never seen television before and were intrigued. Thousands immediately bought sets, and the number of viewers increased by millions a year. The age of television came in with a flourish.

Right: Viewers watching the first televised pictures.

Top left: The world's first outside television broadcast vehicle.

Top right: A television picture of Queen Elizabeth II, wearing her crown and robes,
    About 20 million people watched the Coronation Ceremony on hired sets or on screens set up in public buildings. Few people at this time had their own sets.

Bottom right: Important events can now be transmitted 'live' to our homes, in colour. Colour television was first introduced in 1953, in the U.S.A. It was first used in Britain in 1967, on BBC 2, for Wimbledon. By November 1969, all stations were transmitting in colour.

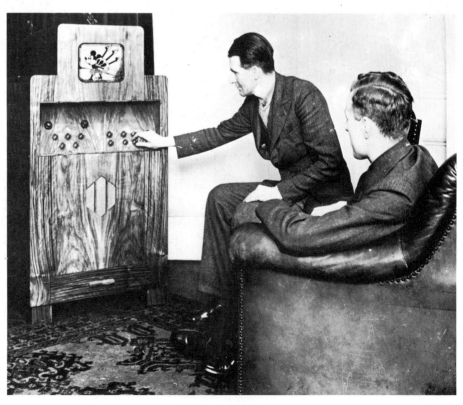

66

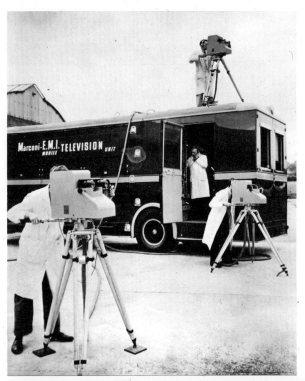

Alexander Fleming

Penicillin: the first antibiotic drug 1928

For more than fifty years after Pasteur's discovery of germs doctors and scientists in many countries tried to produce an antiseptic that could safely be used *internally* for the prevention or cure of bacterial diseases.

Joseph Lister's antiseptic system could prevent external poisoning, as in the case of surgical wounds, but it was not able to destroy bacteria if poisoning had already set in, and it could not cure deep-seated internal infections.

The blood stream contains a mass of minute red and white cells, called corpuscles. All the antiseptics of that time were actually dangerous for internal use because they damaged the white corpuscles. The red corpuscles, which greatly outnumber the white and give the blood its colour, carry oxygen from the lungs to all parts of the body. The white corpuscles provide a natural protection against germs, and their job is to attack and destroy invading microbes. Any antiseptic that damaged these protective cells in the blood stream was therefore likely to do more harm than good.

The problem was to produce a drug with the power to destroy bacteria and yet be harmless to the white corpuscles – an antibiotic drug. All attempts failed. Then, by chance, Alexander Fleming, Professor of Bacteriology at St Mary's Hospital in London, discovered penicillin.

A chance experiment

The story began in 1922 when Fleming, a quiet and keenly observant Scotsman, was 41. One day, while engaged in some bacterial research, Fleming had a bad attack of catarrh and kept blowing his nose. He examined the mucus on his handkerchief and, out of curiosity, he conducted an experiment with his nasal secretions. He put some mucus in a dish containing a culture jelly made from seaweed, in which colonies of microbes were breeding. Next day, he found that the colonies were smaller, indicating that the microbes were gradually fading away. Excited by this discovery, Fleming diluted some mucus and poured the fluid on a mass of bacterial jelly. To his astonishment, the microbes were completely destroyed in a few minutes.

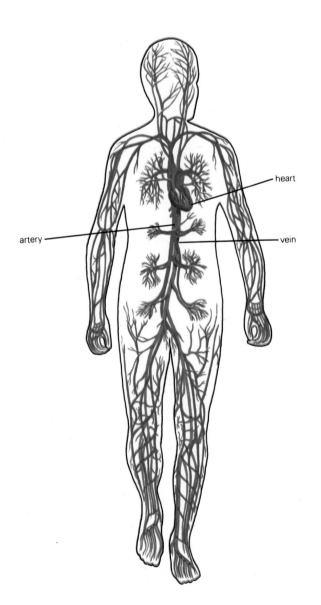

Left: The human blood circulatory system. The heart pumps blood round the body through the arteries (blue). These divide into smaller vessels and tiny capillaries, which supply all the cells, and merge into the venules, or vein endings. The venules lead into larger veins (red), through which the blood returns to the heart.

Right: This gloomy little laboratory at St Mary's Hospital, London, was the scene of Fleming's great discovery.

Fleming then made some tests with other secretions. His eyes were streaming from his catarrh, and he applied some of his tears to bacteria. The microbes vanished in thirty seconds. Fleming coughed up and tested some sputum, and it was equally destructive.

From the results of these experiments, Fleming concluded that the secretions contained an antiseptic that provided a natural protection against germs. He called this mysterious germ-killing substance 'lysozyme' from the medical word 'lyse', meaning to destroy. Inspired by this exciting revelation, Fleming set to work to find a similar substance in some other form of living matter that could be used for the treatment of disease.

Six long years passed, and he made no progress. Then one day in September 1928 something quite unexpected happened. Fleming was conducting some germ experiments in his laboratory – a miserable, gloomy little room – at St Mary's Hospital. He took the cover off a dish of jelly to study the results. Some mould from a plant blew in through the open window and settled on the jelly. To Fleming's surprise and delight, the mould destroyed the microbes in the dish in much the same way as the lysozyme had destroyed bacteria in his earlier experiments.

But for his experiments with his nasal secretions, Fleming 'would have thrown the dish away with appropriate language!' as he said later. Instead, he cultivated the mould by a chemical process and tested it on various types of bacteria. He found that its power to destroy microbes was much greater than that of the lysozyme.

Mould from a plant was blown in through an open window to settle on one of Fleming's culture dishes. The penicillin mould (*inset*) was the result.

Below: Fleming (*left*) receives a joint award with Florey for the discovery of penicillin.

Fleming's next step was to convert the substance into a liquid drug, for the purpose of carrying out some injection tests on diseased animals. He planted some mould in meat broth and left it there for a week. At the end of the week, the broth was covered with a yellow scum but, under the scum, the liquid was clear. Fleming strained the liquid, tested it on some bacterial jelly, and found that it was just as powerful as the original mould.

Florey and Chain

Now came the vital question: would the drug damage the white blood corpuscles if used internally? Fleming injected some diseased rabbits and mice with strong doses. The drug cured their diseases, and the white corpuscles remained strong and healthy.

Fleming had discovered the first completely safe antibiotic drug for the prevention and cure of bacterial diseases – one of the most important discoveries in the history of medicine. He called the new drug 'penicillin' because the mould came from the plant *Penicillium*.

Great as was his achievement, Fleming's battle was not over. He now faced another great problem. Penicillin could not be put to practical use in its raw state, because it quickly loses strength and becomes ineffective. Fleming tried to find some way to purify and concentrate the drug and thereby preserve its strength, but this was beyond his power as he was not a chemist. With great reluctance, Fleming abandoned the task and hoped that one day a skilled chemist might solve the problem.

Nine years passed. It seemed as if Fleming's great discovery might come to nothing. Then, in 1937, Professor Howard Florey, an Australian scientist, and Dr Chain, a German-born chemist, who were engaged in chemical researches in Oxford, took up the work. They studied the chemistry of penicillin – and, after four years of intensive research and experiment, they eventually succeeded in concentrating the drug which is still used for treatment today.

They achieved this in 1941 – the darkest days of the Second World War. Pharmaceutical firms in Britain and America manufactured penicillin on a large scale, and the new antibiotic drug saved the lives of thousands of British and American soldiers, sailors, airmen and others who were wounded in the war.

By his discovery of penicillin, Fleming established a new department of medicine – antibiotics – which led to the development of a wide range of life-saving drugs, in use today.

Fleming was knighted and he, Florey and Chain were jointly awarded the Nobel prize for medicine. Fleming was showered with honours from all over the world, but he was very modest about his achievements. 'Everywhere I go people thank me for saving their lives,' he once remarked. 'I didn't do anything. Nature makes penicillin – I only found it.' Indeed, Fleming seemed to be embarrassed by the praise and publicity.

'Look at him!' said an admirer. 'He's famous and loaded with honours and yet he never tries to be great. He goes on being what he always was.'

Alexander Fleming died from a sudden heart attack in 1955, at the age of 73.

Left: The mould *Penicillium*, as seen under a microscope.

Right: The manufacture of penicillin by means of fermentation tanks at a British factory. During the Second World War, Sir Howard Florey, Dr Chain, and a team of assistants worked out the processes necessary for large-scale production of the antibiotic. Two other antibiotics, salversan, discovered by Ehrlich in 1910, and prontosil, the discovery of Domagk in 1935, were being developed at the same time.

Robert Watson-Watt

Radar: the early warning system 1935

In 1934 Adolph Hitler, the Nazi dictator, came to power in Germany. He determined to expand the German state and began to demand territory from other European countries. The clouds of the Second World War (1939–45) were gathering.

To show their strength, the Nazis claimed that they had developed a deadly radio wave that could kill masses of people, blow up tanks and aircraft, and destroy towns and cities.

Britain was not prepared for war, and the British government were alarmed. They feared that the powerful German air force – the *Luftwaffe* – would attack Britain in great strength and cause terrible death and destruction. So the government asked Robert Watson-Watt, a leading radio expert, to develop a similar radio wave to destroy German aeroplanes in the air – before they could reach Britain.

Watson-Watt, who was a Scotsman, was 43 and he had studied radio waves for many years. He told the government that no waves could destroy aircraft but he believed he could invent a radio instrument to detect aircraft – *radar* (*Ra*dio *D*etection *and R*anging). The instrument would keep a watch on the sky and give a continuous picture of all aeroplanes flying towards Britain, and this early warning system would give the Royal Air Force a chance to fly out to sea and drive back the *Luftwaffe*.

Watson-Watt casually scribbled a few notes and made some rough drawings, and submitted his plans to the government. A modest man, he did not expect them to adopt his idea but, to his surprise, the government commissioned him to develop a radar system immediately and appointed a small team of electrical engineers to assist him.

Watson-Watt and his team conducted their experiments in great secrecy near Daventry, not far from Birmingham. They were afraid that through local gossip their activities might reach the ears of the Nazis; so they put the villagers off the scent by telling them they were trying to find a way to stop cars by radio.

The blip on the screen

Seldom can an inventor have made such rapid progress. In less than six weeks Watson-Watt produced a radar instrument. The system is basically quite simple. Powerful transmitters send out a stream of radio waves at the rate of about 1,000 'pulses' per second. These pulses shoot through the air at immense speed until they hit an object. Then they bounce back at the same speed and hit the aerial of the radar. This produces an immediate 'blip' of light on the radar screen, showing the position and distance of the object.

Left: A formation of German bomber aircraft, Heinkel He-111s, in the Battle of Britain.

Top right: Radar detection. The transmitted signals bounce off the object detected, hitting the aerial and producing a blip of light on the screen, showing the position and distance of the object.

Right: Watson-Watt and his team set up their secret experiment in the countryside near Daventry.

The team fitted their radar instrument with its transmitter and aerial into a van, drove to a lonely spot away from prying eyes, and carried out some tests with aircraft. An aeroplane flew towards them, and they detected it by radar at a distance of about 27 kilometres. There were cries of delight when the blip of light appeared on the screen.

The men constructed a much more powerful transmitter and increased the height of the aerial, and with this superior equipment they gradually extended the range of detection. Finally, they tracked an aeroplane about 120 kilometres away.

Triumphantly, Watson-Watt informed the government that he had developed an efficient radar system that could be used in a war. With great urgency a chain of radar stations was constructed along the south and east coasts of England to watch the sky and give early warning of aeroplanes flying towards Britain from Europe.

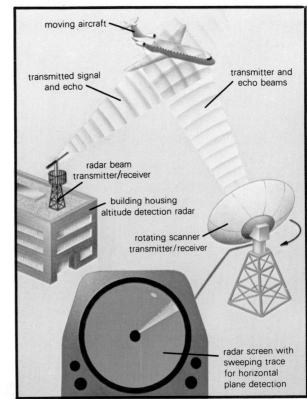

moving aircraft

transmitted signal and echo

transmitter and echo beams

radar beam transmitter/receiver

building housing altitude detection radar

rotating scanner transmitter/receiver

radar screen with sweeping trace for horizontal plane detection

A bird-watching expedition

Suddenly the government received disturbing information. An agent in Europe reported that enormous aerials of an unusual type were being erected in Germany. Were the Germans also developing radar? This was a constant fear. The government immediately sent Watson-Watt on a secret mission to investigate.

Watson-Watt went to Germany with his wife. Posing as holiday-makers on a bird-watching expedition, they dressed in country clothes and went for walks in the districts where the aerials were being erected. Whenever they came to a church with a high tower Watson-Watt climbed to the top and spied the aerials through a small pocket telescope. He decided that they were not radar aerials – but he was wrong. German scientists were beginning to experiment with the idea of radar but they were making little progress – and they never caught up with the British.

As the clouds of war darkened, radar instruments were manufactured on a large scale. The government did not dare tell the manufacturers what they were making as it was vitally important to keep radar secret. To avoid any danger of the secret leaking out, no one firm made a complete instrument. Different firms made different parts, without knowing their purpose, and a team of scientists, sworn to secrecy, then assembled the instruments.

The same strict secrecy also applied to the training of men and women in the use of the radar equipment.

Above: Watson-Watt investigates German radar aerials.

Below: A W.A.A.F. (Women's Auxiliary Air Force) operator uses radar to plot the course of approaching enemy aircraft.

Right: The sinking of the *Scharnhorst*.

When the war broke out in September 1939 Britain was well protected by radar, and soon ships and aircraft were equipped with radar instruments.

Radar was used for the first time in the famous Battle of Britain, in the summer of 1940 – the darkest days of the war, when France was defeated and Britain fought alone. In one day the heroic British fighter pilots, with the aid of radar instruments, tracked and shot down more than 100 German aircraft. By this great victory the Royal Air Force finally won the battle – and saved Britain from invasion.

Throughout the war radar helped Britain and her allies to win many epic battles against heavy odds – in the air, at sea, and on land. One of the greatest naval victories was the sinking of the German battleship *Scharnhorst*. On an inky black night in December 1943 British merchant ships were sailing in the icy Arctic Ocean, transporting war supplies to Russia – and the *Scharnhorst* was preparing to attack them. The battleship was concealed in the darkness, but naval patrol vessels tracked her on their radar screens. They trained their guns on her by radar, and, after a fierce battle, they destroyed the *Scharnhorst*.

Robert Watson-Watt was knighted for his invention and, after the war, he made many technical improvements to the system. He died in 1973.

Today radar comprises highly scientific electronic equipment – far superior to the wartime instruments – and it is used for numerous purposes all over the world. Ships of all nations carry radar to guide them when visibility is poor. Aircraft track their course across the sky with the aid of radar instruments. Police check the speed of motor vehicles on radar screens. Scientists use radar instruments to forecast the weather, to study the stars, and to 'watch' man-made satellites travelling in outer space, far beyond the range of an ordinary telescope.

Radar is as important in peacetime as it was in war – and almost every year the system is used for some new purpose.

Below: Radar antennae fitted below the nose of an R.A.F. Blenheim bomber to detect approaching enemy bombers.

Top right: Shredding aluminium foil. This was dropped by Allied aircraft in an attempt to 'jam' German radar.

Bottom: One of the chain of radar aerials, set up on the coast of Britain to detect low-flying aircraft.

Below: Radar screens situated in Wellington, New Zealand, showing signals picked up from the weather, and surrounding mountains and buildings.

Right: The Royal Navy's H.M.S. *Invincible*, showing surveillance and tracing radar aerials.

Bottom: A modern radar screen with four colour display in use at London's Heathrow Airport. The screen picks up the speed, height, direction and call sign of planes in the area.

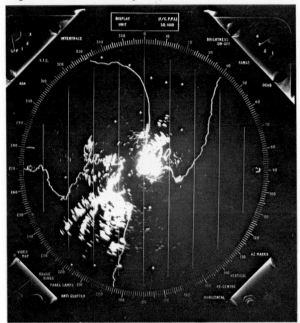

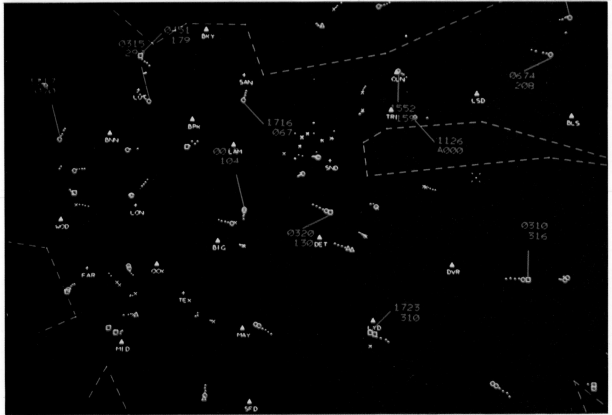

Willem Kolff

Artificial kidney machines 1945

During the last fifty years sensational advances have been made in the treatment of disease, amounting to a medical revolution. Fleming's discovery of penicillin led, as we have seen, to the development of a wide range of life-saving antibiotic drugs. Other drugs have been discovered to prevent crippling diseases such as poliomyelitis. Now, by 'spare parts surgery' it is possible to remove diseased organs of the body and replace them by transplanting healthy organs from other people or by artificial organs.

One of the most important developments was the invention of the kidney machine by Willem Kolff, a Dutch doctor, who was born at Leiden in 1911.

Kolff, whose father and grandfather were doctors, had not originally wanted to be a doctor himself because he hated seeing people suffering. However he did follow in the family tradition and it was the distress concerning a patient – a young man of 22 – who was dying from kidney disease that gave Kolff the inspiration for his invention.

The incident occurred in 1940 when Kolff, who was then 29, was working at a hospital in Groningen. The mother of the young man visited her son, and Kolff had to steel himself to tell her that he was going to die. The poor peasant woman was so upset that Kolff desperately tried to find some way of saving her son's life.

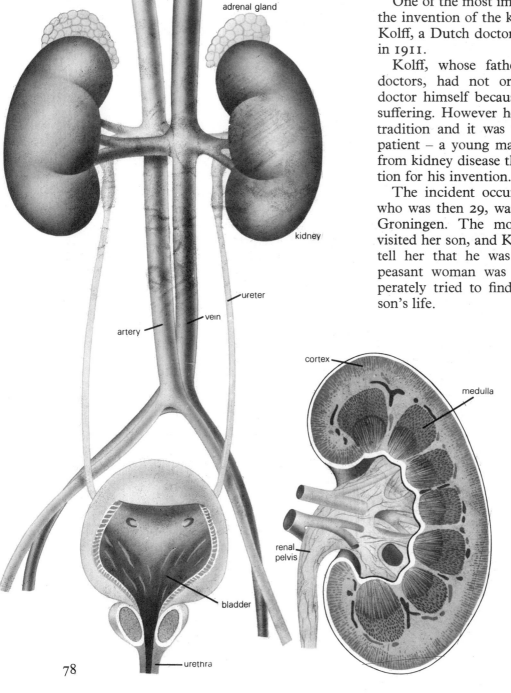

Far left: The urinary system. The kidneys control the amount of salt and water in the body. They remove waste products with the urine they produce. Urine passes down the ureter and is stored in the bladder until it is released through the urethra.

Left: Section taken through a kidney

Right: Blood donating and transfusions. A pint of blood is taken from each donor. The blood is stored according to blood group. When a casualty is brought in, a transfusion of the correct blood type can quickly be carried out, to replace lost blood and save the patient's life.

Above: A Dutch woman, the first patient whose life was saved by a kidney machine. The photograph was taken shortly after the dialysis treatment.

War-time work

The function of the kidneys is to cleanse the blood of impurities and remove the waste matter with the urine. The young man's failing kidneys were not fulfilling this function. Kolff thought: 'If I could remove every day as much waste matter as should normally be excreted with the urine, this man might survive.' He searched through medical books for a way to cleanse the blood and he made some laboratory experiments, but it was all in vain. The young man died.

War then came. On 10 May 1940 the German armies invaded Holland and planes flew over The Hague and dropped leaflets calling on the Dutch to surrender. Kolff and his wife, Janke, who happened to be in The Hague to attend a funeral, watched the Dutch shooting at the German planes – and joined in the applause when one plane caught fire and the crew baled out.

Kolff feared that the Germans might later bomb the city. He did not go to the funeral. Instead, he went to the hospital and offered to set up a blood bank to save the lives of air raid victims. Two armed soldiers drove him round the city on a quest for blood donors, and Kolff established the first blood bank in Europe.

Soon after the German invasion a Dutchman who supported the Nazis was appointed head of the Groningen hospital. Refusing to work for a traitor, Kolff immediately left and went to a hospital at Kampen, by the River Yssel.

Kolff resumed his kidney experiments, and his experience in handling blood *outside* the body when he set up the blood bank now benefited him. He discovered a way to remove the impurities by an experiment with some sausage skin. Kolff put some blood into a tube of sausage skin and immersed it in a saline bath – a salt solution. The waste matter seeped through the thin, porous skin, and in about half an hour the blood was cleansed of all impurities.

Based on this successful experiment, Kolff designed a kidney machine in the form of a revolving drum. Cellophane tubing (similar to sausage skin) was wrapped round the drum, and it rotated in a saline bath. When the machine was connected to the patient his blood passed through the tubing and, as the drum revolved, the impurities seeped through the cellophane. The purified blood then passed out of the machine and returned to the patient.

Secret manufacture

Kolff now had to find a manufacturer to construct his kidney machine. This was very difficult because the Nazis forbade all Dutch industries to work for anyone except the Germans – and any man who disobeyed their orders was in danger of being sent to a forced labour camp in Germany. In spite of the dangers, Kolff persuaded a director of an enamel factory to undertake the work. Working in great secrecy, technicians at the factory constructed the machine and secretly delivered it to Kolff.

Kolff treated his first kidney patient – a young housemaid – but she died. He treated 14 more patients, and they all died. Nevertheless, the kidney machine brought about a temporary improvement in the condition of each patient and this gave Kolff encouragement.

The other doctors at the hospital scoffed and ridiculed his invention, but Kolff ignored their criticisms. A man with a strong will and great determination, Kolff persevered and at last, after striving for nearly two years, he achieved success.

In 1945 Kolff saved the life of a woman who was dying of kidney disease and almost on the point of death. (The woman was permanently cured and lived to an old age.) Kolff went on and saved the lives of several more people.

Delighted by the success of his machine, Kolff decided to give his invention to the world. Eight kidney machines were secretly manufactured and concealed from the Nazis until the end of the war. When peace returned, Kolff gave the machines to England, America, Canada and other countries.

Kolff's system was widely acclaimed by the medical profession and, in the course of time, it was adopted throughout the world. Great technical advances have been made over the years and there are now several types of kidney machine, but the basic principle of the system remains the same.

Left: The first artificial kidney machine, invented by Kolff, consisting of four rotating drums. It was built in great secrecy during the Nazi occupation of Holland.

Top right: A REDY portable recirculating dialysate system, reference by courtesy of Organon Teknika Limited.

Right: A diagram of the working of a modern kidney machine. The patient's blood is passed through an artificial kidney, where the body's waste products are transferred through a special membrane to the dialysate solution. The cleansed blood returns directly to the patient, and the dialysate is then cycled through the sorbent system for cleansing, regenerating and monitoring before returning to the artificial kidney. This process is called haemodialysis.

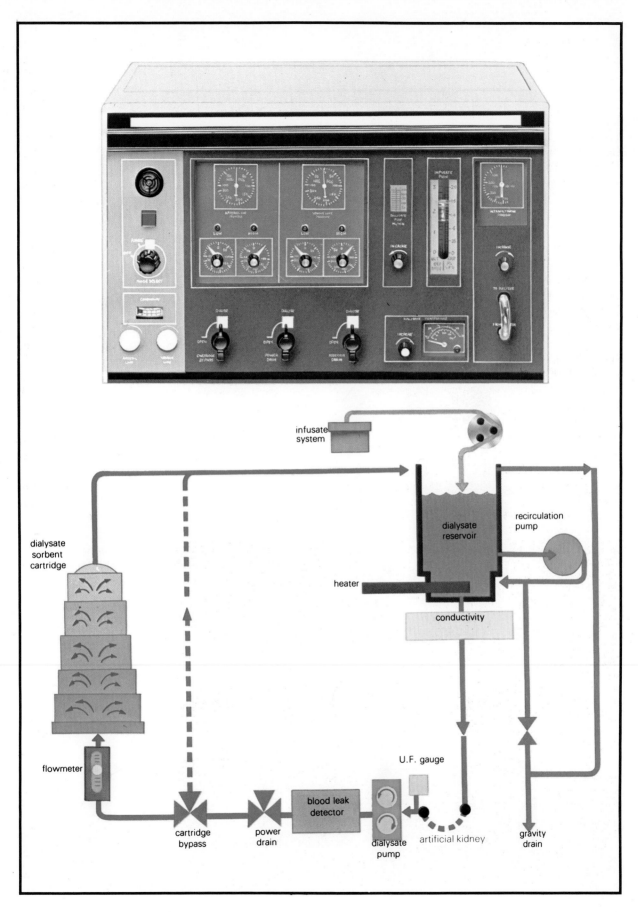

infusate
system

dialysate
sorbent
cartridge

dialysate
reservoir

recirculation
pump

heater

conductivity

flowmeter

cartridge
bypass

power
drain

blood leak
detector

dialysate
pump

U.F. gauge

artificial kidney

gravity
drain

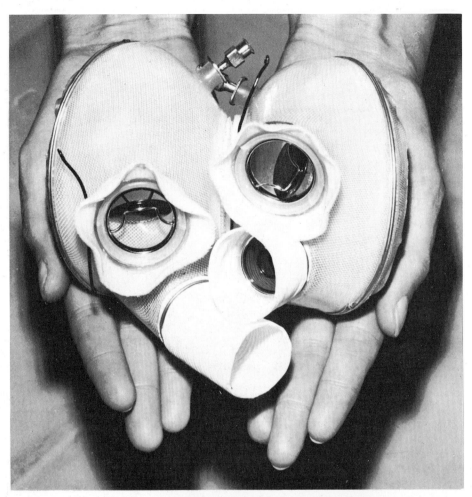

Left: A complete artificial heart, developed at the University of Utah.

Below: This blind patient has been fitted with an artificial eye. The device consists of electrodes implanted in the visual centre of the brain, and a small computer which transmits messages to the brain by stimulating the electrodes. The patient is able to distinguish the horizontal and vertical lines of a television picture.

Right: This patient is harnessed to a small portable artificial kidney machine. Modern machines can be made small enough to fit into the boot of a car, weighing less than 20 kg, and can even be taken on aeroplanes.

Bottom right: Kolff demonstrates a portable, wearable kidney machine on a television programme.

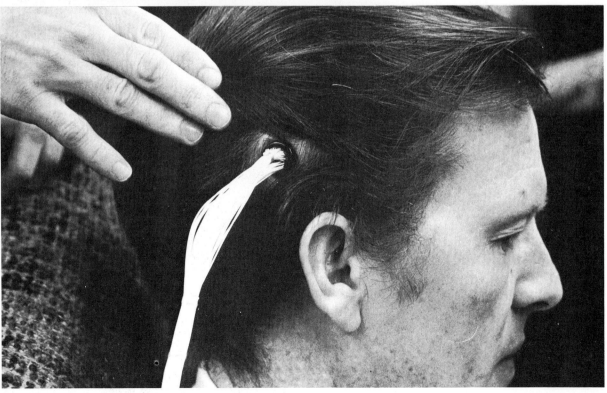

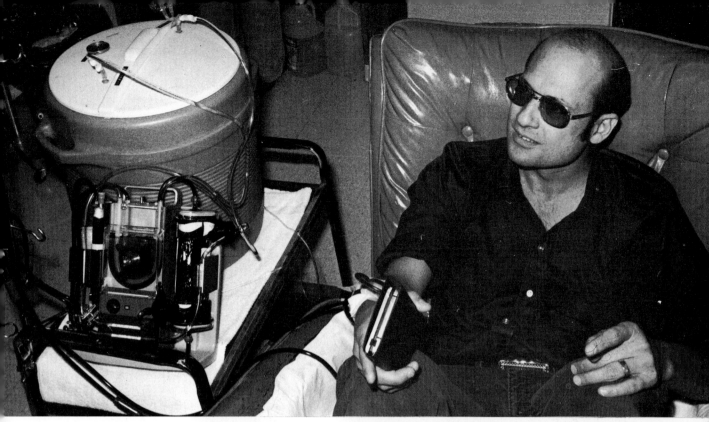

Today hundreds of thousands of people with kidney diseases who would have died are being kept alive through Kolff's invention – and a great many are able to lead a normal life.

Kolff's work for humanity has not ended. In 1950 he emigrated to America and now, at the age of nearly 70, he is professor of Surgery and head of the artificial organs department of Utah University, in Salt Lake City. Working with different groups of scientists and doctors – whom he calls his 'boys' – Kolff is endeavouring to expand 'spare parts surgery' into other fields of medicine.

He has invented an artificial heart, operated by compressed air, which he hopes may give new life to people suffering from heart diseases – the most common cause of death. Kolff, who has a farm for a hobby, transplanted an artificial heart in a dying calf, and the beast revived and lived for six months. The calf died when it grew too big for its heart.

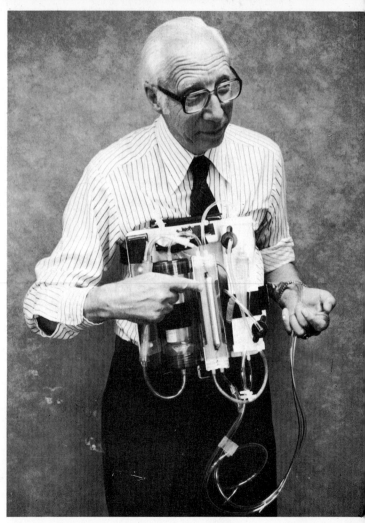

Another ambitious project of Kolff's is the invention of an artificial eye to enable blind people to see. Kolff believes that a tiny television camera, implanted in the eye socket, will transmit pictures to the brain and thereby give a blind person some vision. Fantastic as this idea may seem, Kolff has proved that it is not impossible. He implanted 'eyes' in a totally blind man – and he was able to see blurry images.

Kolff's inventive mind has always been active and seeking new horizons.

Wernher von Braun

The race to the moon 1969

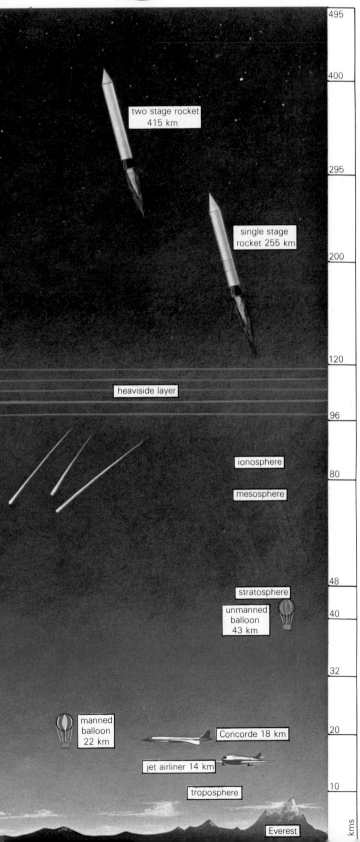

495

400

two stage rocket
415 km

295

single stage
rocket 255 km

200

120

heaviside layer

96

ionosphere

80

mesosphere

48

stratosphere

unmanned
balloon
43 km

40

32

manned
balloon
22 km

Concorde 18 km

20

jet airliner 14 km

troposphere

10

Everest

kms

One of the most sensational events in history was the first landing of men on the moon, on 20 July 1969.

The idea of sending men to the moon was first suggested towards the end of the last century by the famous French writer Jules Verne, who wrote a book called *From the Earth to the Moon*. People laughed at the idea and said it was impossible, but a few far-sighted scientists gave serious thought to the subject.

The moon is about half a million kilometres from the earth. The first great problem was how to construct a rocket to send a spacecraft into space. The rocket would need great power to break through the earth's atmosphere – the gases round the earth – and it must travel at immense speed to overcome the pull of gravity of the sun as otherwise it would crash into it and be destroyed.

Early rockets

At that time rockets used solid fuels and had very little power. An American scientist, Dr Robert Goddard, experimented with liquid fuels to increase their power. His first rocket climbed a mere 14 metres and stayed in the air for two seconds. Eventually Goddard built a rocket that reached an altitude of 2,250 metres, and thereby proved the advantage of liquid fuels.

Then in 1930 a German scientist named Hermann Oberth, who was also experimenting with rockets, wrote an article on the possibilities of space travel – and this captured the imagination of Wernher von Braun, an engineering student in Berlin.

The son of a rich baron, von Braun was 18 years old – young and adventurous. He was intrigued by the mysteries of space, and Oberth's article fired him, he said, 'with a romantic urge to soar through the heavens and explore the mysterious universe'.

Left: The different layers of the Earth's atmosphere, showing the maximum heights reached by single and two stage rockets, balloons, and aeroplanes. The highest point reached by man alone is 8 882 m, the summit of Everest. At that height, the air is so thin that Hillary and Tenzing, the first climbers to conquer Everest, needed oxygen masks to help them breathe.

Above: Hermann Oberth (left) who, in 1931, designed and constructed one of the first successful rockets, powered by liquid fuel. The success of his venture inspired von Braun to build a long range rocket which would send men to the moon.

Right: The launch of one of the test rockets designed by von Braun, near Berlin.

He watched some of Oberth's experiments — and decided to take up the challenge and make some experiments himself. '*I* will build a rocket to send men to the moon,' he declared with complete confidence.

Von Braun and a few other enthusiastic young students rented a field and an old warehouse on the outskirts of Berlin. Working in almost primitive conditions, they constructed rockets in the warehouse and then launched and tested them in the field. They worked in their spare time for about two years, carrying out some 85 tests, and von Braun gradually increased the power of his rockets.

They now had to find some money to buy materials to continue their experiments. They solved this pressing problem by inviting the public to the launchings of their rockets and charging admission fees.

This had a surprising result of great importance. One day in June 1932 three German army officers came to watch a launching. The test was a dismal failure: the rocket did not even leave the ground. Nevertheless, the officers saw that von Braun's ideas were good. They commissioned him to develop his rocket into a weapon for the army and appointed him chief of an experimental rocket station. This set him on his path.

Von Braun conducted experiments on a large scale, and produced some rocket weapons that were more powerful than the heaviest guns.

During the Second World War (1939–45) von Braun was in charge of Germany's vast rocket station at Peenemünde, on the Baltic Sea. There, he and a team of several hundred engineers developed secret rockets to attack England. Von Braun's heart was not in the war, and the Gestapo – the dreaded Nazi secret police – suspected that he might fly to England and reveal the German plans to the British. They arrested him and put him in prison, but he was soon released because his work was so important to Germany.

Left: Von Braun, with his arm encased in plaster, surrenders to the Allied troops in the Austrian Alps in 1945, after his flight from Peenemünde to avoid capture by the Russians. He was taken to the U.S.A., where he continued his research.

Below: A V2 rocket in a vast underground factory in Germany. Designed by von Braun, this was the world's first long-range rocket.

Right: The Saturn V three stage rocket developed by von Braun and his team, and used in the Apollo programme which culminated in the first moon landing.

After the launch, the outer stages were jettisoned until only the Apollo spacecraft remained.

Man first set foot on the moon only 12 years after the first living creature, a small dog called Laika, was sent into space in November 1957. The first man in space was the Russian Yuri Gagarin, in 1961.

Von Braun's regret

A year or so later von Braun designed the first long-range rocket – the V.2. It could climb to a height of 160 kilometres and travel 320 kilometres at a speed of nearly 6,000 kilometres an hour – and it could carry about a tonne of explosives.

The first V.2. rockets were launched against England in September 1944 and they caused many deaths and great destruction. Von Braun deeply regretted this. 'I designed the rocket to blaze the trail to other planets – not to destroy our own,' he said.

When the war was coming to an end, von Braun and about 100 other German engineers packed the secret plans of the V.2. rocket and escaped from Peenemünde in lorries. After a hazardous journey, dodging German troops, they reached the advancing American forces and gave themselves up.

The American officers who interrogated von Braun did not believe that he was really the inventor of the V.2. 'He seems too young and too jovial,' they said. However, von Braun eventually convinced them.

After the war the German team went to America and von Braun spent the next few years developing longer-range rockets, based on the V.2., for the American army – but all the time his eyes were focussed on the moon.

The Russian lead

Meanwhile, the Russians were also producing rockets, and in 1957 they launched the first unmanned satellite, *Sputnik I*, into space.

This was a bitter blow for von Braun. He persuaded the United States Government to take up the challenge and allow him to build space rockets. The Government established a great space flight centre at Houston, Texas, and appointed von Braun director.

A race for the moon between America and Russia began.

In 1961 the Russians scored another triumph and sent the first man into space – Yuri Gagarin. But, great as this achievement was, Gagarin travelled only round the earth.

A rocket with a much longer range was needed to shoot a spacecraft into *outer* space, where the moon lies. It seemed impossible to produce a single rocket with sufficient power, but von Braun and his team eventually solved the problem by developing a rocket with three separate sections, called 'stages' – the Saturn 5 rocket.

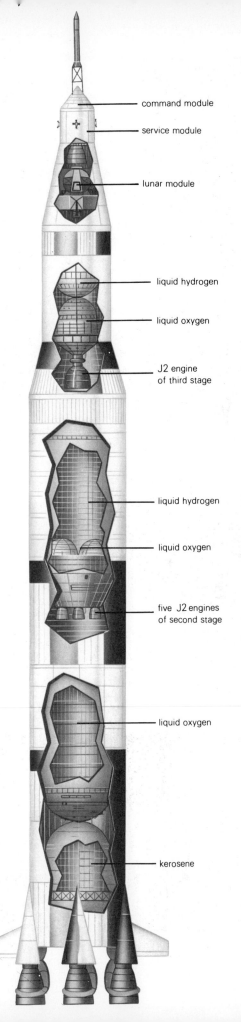

command module

service module

lunar module

liquid hydrogen

liquid oxygen

J2 engine
of third stage

liquid hydrogen

liquid oxygen

five J2 engines
of second stage

liquid oxygen

kerosene

The spacecraft sat in the nose, and each section, containing powerful engines, drove the rocket in turn. The tail section launched the rocket into the sky, and then fell away. The engines of the middle section took over and drove the rocket to a much greater height, and then likewise burnt up. As each section fell away, the weight was naturally reduced and the speed of the rocket therefore increased. Finally, the last engines burnt up – and the spacecraft travelled through space alone by its own velocity.

With the three-stage Saturn 5, von Braun finally achieved his life's ambition to build a rocket to send men to the moon.

Meanwhile, teams of scientists and engineers designed and constructed various types of spacecraft, and American astronauts carried out numerous daring test flights in space to study conditions in space. Preparations for the great event were immense and extended over several years.

At last, in July 1969, came the great day for man's attempt to conquer the moon. Von Braun's giant rocket was set up on a launching site at Cape Canaveral, in Florida. In the nose of the rocket sat the great spacecraft *Apollo 11*, which contained a detachable landing unit

called *Eagle*. Three American astronauts – Neil Armstrong, Edwin Aldrin and Michael Collins – climbed into the spacecraft and waited anxiously for the 'lift-off'.

Tense with anxiety, von Braun watched the launching. With a roar, the rocket shot into the sky. The three stages burnt out in turn – and Apollo travelled through space alone at a speed of 40,000 kilometres an hour.

The long and dangerous journey in space lasted four days. At last, they reached the moon. Collins stayed in Apollo, and Armstrong and Aldrin climbed into the landing unit *Eagle*. They fired the engine and began to descend. Their descent was extremely dangerous but they survived the hazards – and landed safely on the moon.

The moon landing caused intense excitement throughout the world. One of the happiest men was von Braun, who had lived for this day.

Eight years after this historic landing, in 1977, von Braun died of cancer.

Below: The American Apollo 11 astronauts, Neil Armstrong and Edwin Aldrin, who made the first moon landing, and Michael Collins (*centre*) who remained in the command module.

Right: One of the astronauts on the moon.

88

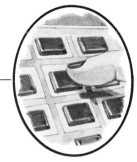

The Computer Age

Charles Babbage and his successors

The invention which is making some of the biggest changes in our lives today is the computer. The computer evolved from hand-operated adding machines and it was given its name because its purpose is to calculate, or *compute*, mathematical problems.

An Englishman, Charles Babbage, designed the first computer in 1833. It was an immense machine, containing thousands of moving parts, and the cost of construction was £23,000. The project was abandoned because the machine was too complicated – but Babbage's idea was brilliant and gave the lead to others.

A Swedish scientist, George Scheutz, designed a simpler machine on the same principle, and an Englishman, Bryan Donkin, then modified his design. Donkin's computer was used by an insurance company to calculate and compile tables for insurance policies.

In 1889 Dr Herman Hollerith, a German living in America, took a great step forward and invented an electrically-operated 'data-processing' computer with a code system comprising patterns of holes punched on cards. A card containing coded information was fed into the machine, and the machine printed the data on tape by means of electrical impulses generated by the holes. Hollerith's computer was much faster than previous machines, and the 'punched card' system is still widely used today.

Nearly 60 years passed. Then a new field opened up – electronics – and the electronic computer was born. In 1946 American engineers at Pennsylvania University first designed a machine combining electronics with electromagnetic devices. Technical developments quickly followed and five years later, in 1951, the first all-electronic computers were produced by firms in Britain and America.

The modern electronic computer operates almost automatically, and millions of times faster than the old mechanical machines. It is a very complex machine – really a combination of machines – and the various parts do different jobs: calculating and recalculating information; feeding in information from the people who use the machine, and printing out information to the people who need it. Many computers have screens, rather like television screens, on which people can see printed information as soon as it has been calculated.

Over the years computers have been getting smaller and smaller, and engineers can now put all the 'circuits' on to tiny elements of chemical material called silicon chips: the entire wiring of a computer can be 'printed' on to a piece of material much smaller than a fingernail. This means that tiny computers, called 'microprocessors', can be built into all sorts of machines in everyday use.

The computer can fulfil numerous functions – calculate mathematical problems; compile accounts; print and transmit messages; or operate machines in factories. Its functions extend beyond the earth into space. On the expeditions to the moon, computers in the Apollo spacecraft transmitted a continuous operational report to the control centre at Houston and, if any fault occurred, the controllers were able to correct it from the ground by other computers.

Industries and businesses throughout the world use computers extensively to save time and labour, and thereby reduce costs. The 'electronic brain' is transforming business methods and industrial practice on a scale comparable with the Industrial Revolution.

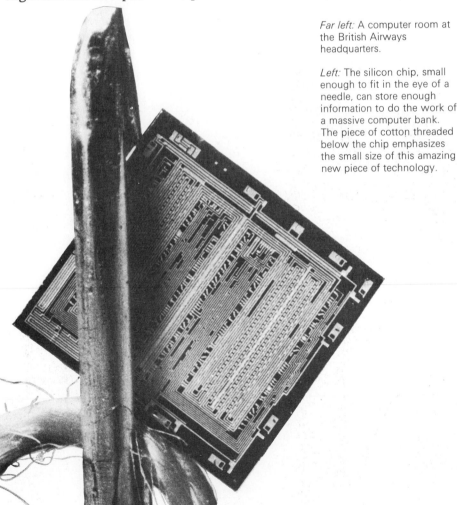

Far left: A computer room at the British Airways headquarters.

Left: The silicon chip, small enough to fit in the eye of a needle, can store enough information to do the work of a massive computer bank. The piece of cotton threaded below the chip emphasizes the small size of this amazing new piece of technology.

Index

1 2 3 4 5 6 7 8 9 10—U—90 89 88 87 86 85 84 83 82